A Mathematical Accounting Model

and its MathAccounting Software

Guoping Jie

A Mathematical Accounting Model and its MathAccounting Software

First Edition

ISBN: 0995820309

ISBN-13: 978-0995820302 (Guoping Jie)

WWW.mathaccounting.com

Acknowledgements

I wish to take this opportunity to sincerely thank OSAP system (Canada) which gave me a chance to study.

Guoping Jie

After graduating from the Beijing University of Aeronautics and Astronautics, I immediately went to The National University of Defense Technology in Changsha, China. Three years later, I got my master degree and went to Shanghai XinLi Machinery Factory where I design and develop motors as an engineer. In 2005, I immigrated to Canada with my child after having worked for many years. In 2007, I entered the Centennial College, Toronto, Canada to study accounting. During two years, I had had some thinking about accounting and its software. I went to the York University, Toronto, Canada in 2009 and graduated with the Honors BAS four years later. After having taken many years to research and develop mathematical accounting model and its MathAccounting software, I opened the Foreverr MathAccounting Software Company Ltd. in February, 2015.

For relaxation, I enjoy reading, driving, and travelling.

ABSTRACT

It should be time to study and apply a mathematical accounting model which is easy to understand and audit, and is accurate and reliable. The paper distinctly describes three accounting's concepts or models (physical accounting model, double-entry system model, and mathematical accounting model) and their relationships. The physical accounting model naturally exists since business emerging and is the basis of all other accounting models. The physical accounting model is actually consisted of every transaction which is based on a principle: exchange of equal values. The double-entry system model, which is still used all over the world, uses a logical method to keep recording transactions accurate. Its main characters are the T account with debit and credit, chart of accounts, two classes of permanent and temporary accounts, and trial balance. The mathematical accounting model is based on a basic expanding accounting equation and has developed following main characters: mathematical axiom principle, dynamic accounting equation, sub-equation of the dynamic accounting equation, five classes of permanent accounts, multi-subaccount name, structures of financial statements, and account flow statement. The same parts of the double-entry system and mathematical accounting models are to satisfy the basic accounting equation at the beginning of a fiscal year and the ending of a fiscal year, but the difference of them is that they take the different ways to reach the ending of the fiscal year. Based on the mathematical accounting model, I have developed a MathAccounting software. The MathAccounting software has four function models: Transactions, Reports, Backup/Restore, and Maintenances. The MathAccounting software has little limitation, so it can be used by all economic entities regardless of their size, nature of business, and form of business organization without any altering. The book also introduces a concept of the great accounting, which is based on the MathAccounting software and the wealth conservation law, in detail. The great accounting means two aspects. In the great data time, centered management of accounting is an inexorable trend. Every business company can login in a government's centered database by using of its business number. And every department in an organization can do part work of the accounting about itself duty. All works of the organization's departments will be made up of the financial statements. The great accounting has many advantages, such as being difficult to draw up false accounts and to evade a tax.

Keywords: physical accounting model, double-entry system accounting model, mathematical accounting model, MathAccounting software, and great accounting

Contents

Chapter1

Introduction of Mathematical Accounting Model

It should be time to study and apply a mathematical accounting model which is easy to understand and audit, and is accurate and reliable. Meanwhile, accounting students should take a course of database at least, such as SQL Server or Oracle, to understand the mathematical accounting model clearly.

Three important accounting's concepts or models and their relationships can be identified clearly. They are the physical accounting model, the double-entry system model, and the mathematical accounting model.

1.1 Physical accounting model

First, what is the physical accounting model? Since business emerging, the physical accounting model naturally exists. The physical accounting model is the basis of all other accounting's models. It is consisted of every transaction. These transactions are naturally based on a principle: exchange of equal values. By using of mathematical language, each transaction based on this principle means each sub-equation, which actually implies a basic accounting equation:

Assets = Liabilities + Owner's Equity.

1.2 Double-entry system model

For knowing and understanding business performance, people has tried to build many accounting models to record and summarize the economic events in fact, such as an owner of a corner grocery store who might use a very simple accounting model to record his or her transactions. Just like a saying that all roads lead to Rome.

Without effective computing tools, the double-entry system model actually uses a logical method to keep recording transactions accurate, so this double-entry system accounting model has gradually become popular in the world and is still used all over the world now. It has following main characters:

- T account with debit and credit. The principle of exchange of equal values implies that the sum of the debit is equal to the sum of the credit in a transaction here.
- Chart of accounts. It is a framework for entire database of the current accounting software.
- Permanent and temporary accounts. All accounts are divided into two classes of accounts: permanent and temporary accounts. The Assets, Liabilities, and Owner's equity are the permanent accounts. The Revenues and Expenses are the temporary accounts which will be closed at the end of every fiscal year and be merged into the Owner's Equity in the basic accounting equation. Its basic accounting equation is: Assets = Liabilities + Owner's Equity
- The basic accounting equation with rules and effects on each type of account:

    Assets = Liabilities   +   Owner's Equity

    Assets = Liabilities + Capital − Drawings + Revenues - Expenses

Dr.	Cr.	Dr.	Cr.	Dr.	Cr.	Dr.	Cr.	Dr.	Cr.	Dr.	Cr.
+	-	-	+	-	+	-	+	-	+	+	-

- General journal.
- Posting to ledger.
- Trial balance. The trial balance calculation is an obvious symbol of deviating from the basic accounting equation because the amount of the total debit or total credit is normally not equal to the amount of the total assets or the sum of the total liabilities and total equity (the two sides' amounts of the dynamic accounting equation). The double-entry system only checks the recording information by using of the basic accounting equation at the end of a fiscal year.

1.3 Mathematical accounting model

Last concept is the mathematical accounting model. In the mathematical accounting model, it is very important that the basic accounting equation must be an expanding form:

Assets = Liabilities + Equity + Incomes − Expenses

Based on this equation, the mathematical accounting model has been developed following main characters:

- Mathematical axiom principle.
- Dynamic accounting equation.
- Sub-equation of dynamic accounting equation. Every transaction is a sub-equation which is also called general equation.
- Five classes of the accounts. All accounts are divided into five classes of the accounts which are all the permanent accounts and have same position in the dynamic accounting equation. This concept is very important for developing the mathematical accounting model. The Assets are the first class of accounts, the Liabilities are the second class of accounts, the Equities are the third class of accounts, the Incomes are the fourth class of accounts, and the Expenses are the fifth class of accounts.
- Multi-subaccount name. Its form is the "A3<A2<A1". The A1, the A2, and the A3 are one-level subaccount, two-level subaccount, and three-level subaccount names of a parent account respectively. The three-level subaccount A3 must be unique if a parent account has any three-level subaccount. Obviously, if a parent account has only any two-level subaccount or any one-level subaccount, then the two-level subaccount A2 or the one-level subaccount A1 must be unique too.
- Structures of financial statements.
- Concept of account flows statement.

The mathematical accounting model is based on following mathematical axiom.

If $a + b = c + d$,
        $e + f = g + h$,

Then　　$a + b + e + f = c + d + g + h$

The mathematical axiom is the nucleus and framework of the mathematical accounting model, and is through all process of accounting. Meanwhile, the mathematical axiom also guarantees the recording accounting information correct and accurate.

In the mathematical accounting model, it is a great advantage that the increasing of an account's balance is the "+" and the decreasing of an account's balance is the "-" for all accounts of the assets, liabilities, equities, incomes, and expenses, which is the same as personal habit.

The basic accounting equation is rewritten and categorized, and I get the following dynamic accounting equation.

Assets (1) = Liabilities (2) + Equity (3) + Incomes (4) – Expenses (5)

In the above equation, each class account has many parent accounts, so the dynamic accounting equation can be again rewritten as an expanding dynamic accounting equation.

Assets (1) (Cash + Inventory + …) = Liabilities (2) (Account Payable + Notes Payable + …) + Equity (3) (Share capital + Retained earnings + …) + Incomes (4) (Revenues + Other Revenues + …) – Expenses (5) (Cost of Sales Sold + Interest Expenses + …)

In fact, every transaction is a sub-equation of the dynamic accounting equation. If adding a sub-equation to the previous dynamic accounting equation, then I get a new dynamic accounting equation at a special time point. If you image that the accounting is a straight railway system, then every transaction is a railway sleeper and the train is a dynamic accounting equation and goes ahead. Each account does not need be closed. The financial statements are only the results of the moving and uniting the some terms in the dynamic accounting equation at a special time point.

What is relationship between the double-entry system model and the mathematical accounting model? The Figure 1-1 can clearly show the answer and explain the question.

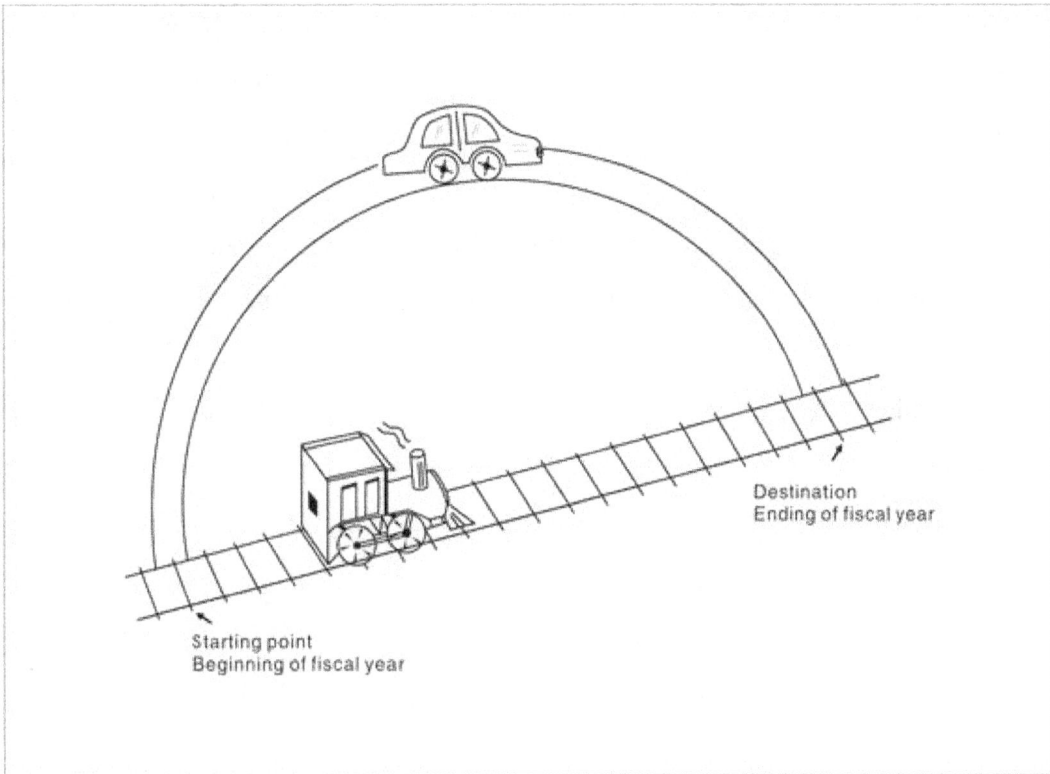

Figure 1-1   Same Parts and Difference of two Accounting Models

If you think that the time of a fiscal year is a stretch of rail, then the starting point of the rail is regarded as the beginning of the fiscal year and the destination of the rail is regarded as the ending of the fiscal year. The same parts of the two accounting models are that the two accounting models satisfy the basic accounting equation at the starting point of the rail (the beginning of the fiscal year) and the destination of the rail (the ending of the fiscal year). However, the two accounting models take the different ways to reach the destination from the starting point.

The mathematical accounting model drives on the rail track all the time until reaching the destination. The train is the dynamic accounting equation. Every railway sleeper is a sub-equation which is also called as a general equation in the MathAccounting software. The train is driving on the railway, which means that every sub-equation is being added to the previous dynamic accounting equation. When the train reaches the destination of the rail, the last dynamic accounting equation is finally gotten at the ending of the fiscal year.

The double-entry system model leaves the rail track at the starting point after all ledger accounts being checked to satisfy the basic accounting equation, and takes the other road to reach the destination. The road is consisted of all T accounts with debit and credit, general journalizing transactions, and chart of accounts which is the framework of this model. The car is consisted of posting to ledger accounts and calculating trial balance. After reaching the destination, all ledger accounts must be checked again to satisfy the basic accounting equation.

In the mathematical accounting model, following five transactions can be written by using five sub-equations.

- Investment by owners. On January 2, 2014, Ping Wang, Hua Li and Mike Newsome decide to open a RR trade business, so Ping Wang invests $4,000 cash in business, and Hua Li and Mike Newsome each invest $3,000 cash in business. The sub-equation can be written as following:

    Cash (1): 10000 = Share capital (3): 4000 + Share capital (3): 3000
    + Share capital (3): 3000

    This sub-equation is also the dynamic accounting equation on January 2, 2014 (in other word, the first dynamic accounting equation is the "0 = 0" for a new company). It can be rewritten as following:

    Cash (1): 10000 = Share capital (3): 10000

- Purchase of the supplies by cash. On January 3, 2014, RR Company purchases some supplies by $193 cash from AA Company. Then the sub-equation is:

    Cash (1): -193 + Supplies (1): 193 = 0

    Adding this sub-equation to the previous dynamic accounting equation, I get a new dynamic accounting equation on January 3, 2014. It is:

Cash (1): 9807 + Supplies (1): 193 = Share capital (3): 10000

- Cash payments for Hua Li's taxi fee expenses. On the same day, Hua Li takes taxi to carry on the supplies by $47 cash. Then the sub-equation is:

    Cash (1): -47 = - Travelling expenses (5): 47

    On the same day, the new dynamic accounting equation after adding this transaction sub-equation is:

    Cash (1):9760 + Supplies (1): 193 = Share capital (3): 10000 - Travelling expenses (5): 47

- Purchase of inventory by some cash and other on credit. On January 5, 2014, RR Company purchases $3,670 inventory by cash -$670 and other on credit from A1 Company (phone number: 987654321). Then the sub-equation is:

    Cash (1): -670 + Inventory (1): 3670 = Account payable (2): 3000

    On January 5, 2014, the new dynamic accounting equation after adding this transaction is:

    Cash (1): 9090 + Supplies (1): 193 + Inventory (1): 3670 = Account payable (2): 3000 + Share capital (3): 10000 - Travelling expenses (5): 47

- Sales for some cash and other on credit. On January 5, 2014, RR Company sells $1,900 inventory to B1 Company (phone number: 123456789) for sales of $2,530, and receives cash 300. Then the sub-equation is:

    Cash (1): 300 +Inventory (1): -1900 + Account receivable (1): 2230 = Sales (4): 2530 - Cost of sales (5): 1900

On the same day, the new dynamic accounting equation after adding this transaction sub-equation is:

Cash (1): 9390 + Supplies (1): 193 + Inventory (1): 1770 + Account receivable (1): 2230 = Account payable (2): 3000 + Share capital (3): 10000 + Sales (4): 2530 − Travelling expenses (5): 47 − Cost of Sales (5): 1900

In a word, the sub-equation of the first transaction is also the dynamic accounting equation on January 2, 2014. Adding the second transaction's sub-equation to this dynamic accounting equation, I get a new dynamic accounting equation on January 3, 2014. Finally, I get a new dynamic accounting equation on January 5, 2014. It is:

Cash (1): 9390 + Supplies (1): 193 + Inventory (1): 1770 + Account receivable (1): 2230 = Account payable (2): 3000 + Share capital (3): 10000 + Sales (4): 2530 − Travelling expenses (5): 47 − Cost of Sales (5): 1900

The total assets are $13,583, and the sum of the liabilities, equity, incomes, and expenses are $13,583 too. By moving and uniting the terms in the dynamic accounting equation at a time point, I can easily get income statements, balance sheet, cash flows statement, and so on.

Real business is more complicate than this example. Moreover, many accounts have multi-level subaccounts, such as the account of the "Travelling Expenses". It may have three-level subaccounts (different persons, different departments, and different factories). In fact, there is obviously an account which has the one-level subaccounts in this example. Do you find it? It is the account of the "Share capital" that is consisted of the three one-level subaccounts of the "Capital-Ping Wang", the "Capital-Hua Li", and the "Capital-Mike Newsome".

For dealing with complicate business, an effective computing tool of the SQL Database or the Oracle Database must be used. For meeting the requirement of the SQL Database or the Oracle Database, the above basic dynamitic accounting equation must be rewritten by using of mathematical language. It is:

X1 = X2 + X3 + X4 - X5

Here the X1 is the Assets, X2 is the Liabilities, X3 is the Equity, X4 is the Incomes, and X5 is the Expenses.

The expanding dynamic accounting equation is:

$$(X11 + X12 + X13 + \ldots) = (X21 + X22 + X23 + \ldots) + (X31 + X32 + X33 + \ldots)$$
$$+ (X41 + X42 + X43 + \ldots) - (X51 + X52 + X53 + \ldots)$$

All terms in the above equation are called the parent accounts, and will appear on the financial statements.

If a parent account, such as the X12, has one-level subaccounts, then its one-level subaccounts are the X121, X122, X123, and so on.

If a parent account, such as the X41, has two-level subaccounts, then its one-level subaccounts are the X411, X412, X413, and so on. The one-level subaccounts may have their two-level subaccounts. For a one-level subaccount, such as the X 412, its two-level accounts are the X4121, X4122, X4123, and so on.

If a parent account, such as the X53, has three-level subaccounts, then its one-level subaccounts are the X531, X532, X533, and so on. For a one-level subaccount, such as the X533, its two-level accounts are the X5331, X5332, X5333, and so on. For a two-level subaccount, such as the X5331, its three-level subaccounts are the X53311, X53312, X53313, and so on. From theory, an account can have the infinite-level subaccounts.

Therefore, the expanding dynamic equation is very huge and very complicate for a company with many three-level subaccounts. You do not worry about that. The computer can do difficult calculation and categorizing work behind the screen in the digital time. You must only understand a basic principle. When a sub-equation, which is the lowest-level sub-equation and is checked to be correct, is added to the previous dynamic accounting equation, all terms of this sub-equation will be added to its relevant parent accounts and upper subaccounts.

There is a problem which must be technically solved. If a parent account X11 has more than 10 one-level subaccounts, such as 22 one-level subaccounts, then its twelfth one-level subaccount X1112 may be confused with a two-level subaccount X1112, whose one-level subaccount and parent account are the X111 and the X1 respectively, by the computer. For resolving the problem, every parent account and its multi-level subaccount are represented by using of two digital numbers if the maximum numbers of them are less than 100.

The expanding dynamic accounting equation is rewritten as:

(X101 + X102 + X103 + … + X199) = (X201 + X202 + X203 + … + X299) + (X301 + X302 + X303 + … + X399) + (X401 + X402 + X403 + … + X499) - (X501 + X502 + X503 + … + X599)

If the parent account X197 has the 99 one-level subaccounts, then its 6th one-level subaccount is the X19706 and the 99th one-level subaccount is the X19799.

The parent accounts will appear on the balance sheet and the income statements, so I design the structures of the balance sheet and income statements, as the Figure 1-2 on the next page.

To design own balance sheet and income statement, a user can enter subtotal name into the big box at the left of the Figure 1-2 and its row number into the right box; the user needs also enter parent account name into the small box at the left of the Figure 1-2 and the account's row number into the right box. Obviously, the two row numbers cannot be same. The two row numbers must not be sequence, but they must be in a scope, such as a scope of 201 to 301. Because each scope is enough for all possible parent accounts, I recommend that the row number of a new subtotal name will be odd number and a new parent account's row number will be even number. If a company has any income that must not pay tax or any expense that cannot be deducted, the user can put them under the parent account of the "Income taxes expenses". Their row numbers should be between 600 and 650.

The subtotal names and the parent account names will appear in the income statements and the balance sheet by the order of the numbers that the user entered.

ASSETS   101

Total assets
LIBILITIES   201

Total liabilities
SHAREHOLDERS' EQUITY   301

Total shareholders' equity
Total liabilities and shareholders' equity

                                                                          401

Total

Total
Gross Margin   451

Total

Total
Earnings Before Income Taxes   551

Total

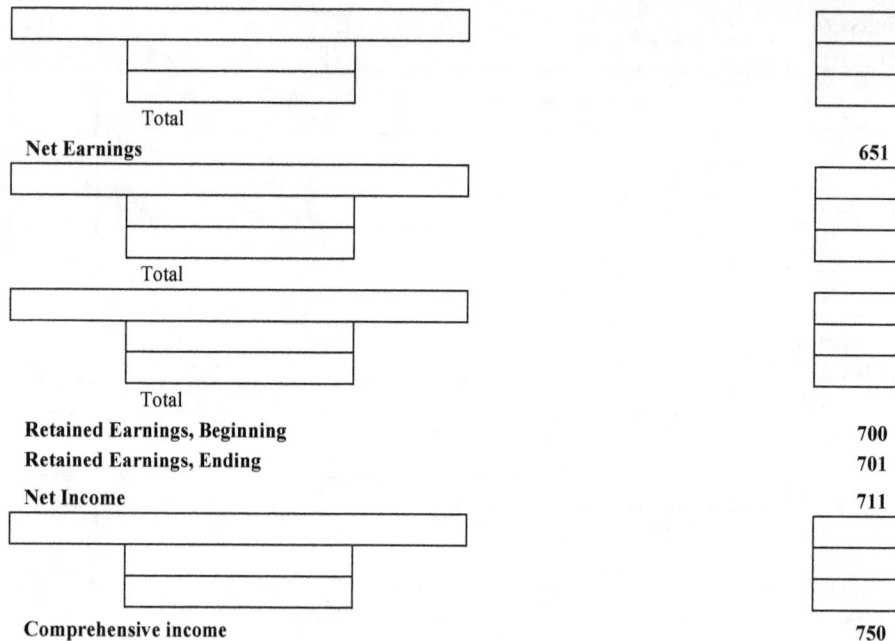

Figure 1-2 Structures of Balance Sheet and Income Statements

For above first transaction, a user can enter a subtotal name of the "Current assets" into the big box at the left of the Figure 1-2 and the number "103" or other appropriate number you like into the right box; the user needs also enter the parent account of the "Cash" into the small box at the left of the Figure 1-2 and its row number "104" or other appropriate number you like into the right box. Then the user can enter a subtotal name of the "Owners' capital" into the big box at the left of the Figure 1-2 and the number "303" or other appropriate number you like into the right box; the user needs also enter the parent account of the "Share capital" into the small box at the left of the Figure 1-2 and the number "304" or other appropriate number you like into the right box.

I can use the tool of the subaccount concept to build cash flows statement. The Figure 1-3, seeing the next page, shows the structure of the cash flows statement.

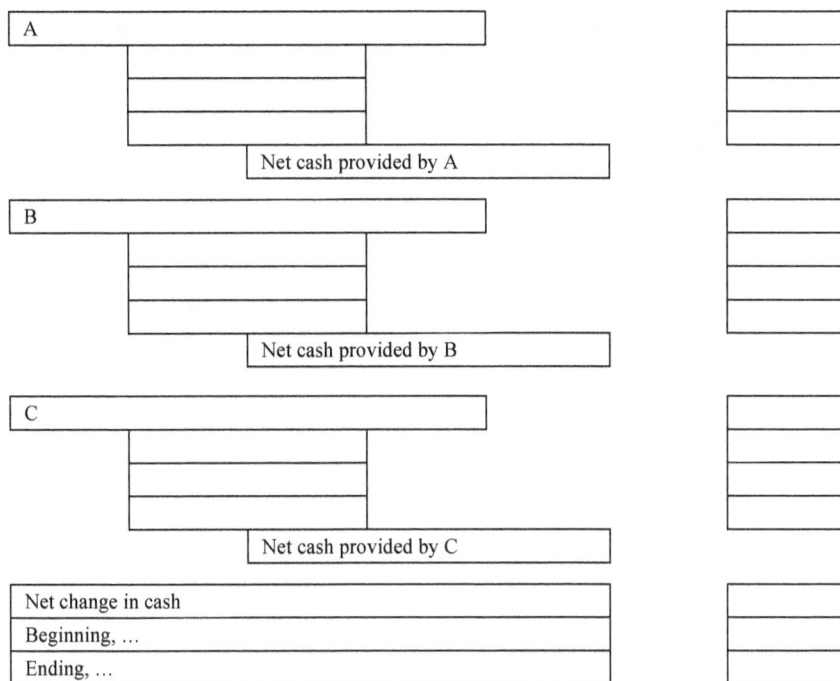

Figure 1-3   Structure of Cash Flow Statement

The cash account has the three one-level subaccounts: operating activities, investing activities, and financing activities. Of course, every one-level subaccount can have the unlimited two-level subaccounts. The contents of the big boxes at the left of the Figure 1-3 are the names of the one-level subaccounts, and the contents of the small boxes at the left of the Figure 1-3 are the names of the two-level subaccounts; the contents of the right boxes are all one-level subaccounts and the two-level subaccounts' balances which can be gotten from the tables which I will create below.

If cash is paid to a supplier for inventory, then its one-level subaccount name is the "Operating activities" and its two-level subaccount name is the "Cash payments to suppliers". If cash is paid for a machine, then its one-level subaccount name is the "Investing activities" and its two-level subaccount name is the "Cash payments of machinery". The one-level subaccounts' names of the "Operating activities" and the "Investing activities" will appear in the A box and the B box respectively. The two-level subaccounts' names of the "Cash payments to suppliers" and the "Cash payments of machinery" will appear in the small boxes under the A box and the B box respectively. So I can design my style of the cash flows statement by using of this structure. At the ending of every fiscal year, I can get the cash flows statement from the tables which I will create below. In fact, I can get the cash flows statement just clicking a box in the MathAccounting software. It is so easy.

From this idea, I can get a new concept of account flows statement if an account has the two-level subaccounts. If number of its one-level subaccounts is more than three, then the top three one-level subaccounts' names according to their balances will appear on the account flow statement.

For account receivable and account payable accounts, they only have different customers and different suppliers respectively. Because each customer or each supplier's telephone number is unique, I can use the tool of subaccount concept again to think that the customers' or suppliers' telephone numbers are the one-level subaccounts' names of the account receivable or the account payable.

So far, a new parent account has following items that a user must enter in a database at most:

- Transaction Date.
- General ID.
- Explanation.
- Class (1-5).
- MultiSubaccount name. Its form is the "A3<A2<A1". Every the lowest subaccount must be sole.
- Amount.
- Subtotal Name (including its row number). Its form is the "subtotal name, its row number".
- Reference (account row number, or account receivable or account payable's General ID).

For a new customer or supplier, the information of customer or supplier's name, address, E-mail, postal code, city, state, and country must also be entered too.

A sample of original proof of a transaction is showed in the Figure 1-4 on the next page. In filling in an original proof, you must change the amounts of the fifth class accounts to the negative amounts.

Transaction Original Proof							
Transaction Date:						General ID	
Explanation:							
No.	Class	Account Name	Left Amount	Right Amount	Multi-subaccount Name	Subtotal Name	Reference
1							
2							
3							
4							
5							
6							
7							
8							
Total							
Customer or Supplier's Name			Address		E-mail		Postal Code
City			State		Country		

Person Handling: Manager:

Date: Date:

Figure 1-4   Original Proof of Transaction

Now, I will show you the process of manually recording the accounting information by using of the mathematical accounting model without the database.

For calculating the parent accounts' and the subaccounts' balances after a transaction, the following steps must be done.

First, a transaction sub-equation must be built after filling in an original proof. Then, the sub-equation must be changed to a mathematical sub-equation.

Second, all subaccounts in this transaction must be identified to build the multi-level sub-equations. All terms or items' amounts in the lowest-level sub-equation can be gotten from the transaction original proof directly.

Third, when the three-level sub-equation is added to the two-level sub-equation or when the two-level sub-equation is added to the one-level sub-equation, the lower level subaccounts' amounts are added to upper level subaccounts' amounts (them belonging to the same parent account). However, the amounts for two same terms must not be added together, which means that their amounts do not change. When the one-level sub-equation is add to the transaction sub-equation, all parent accounts' amounts can respectively be gotten from their related one-level subaccounts.

Finally, for getting the parent accounts' balances after the transaction, the transaction sub-equation must be added to a previous dynamic accounting equation.

For recording the transaction and getting the parent accounts and all related subaccounts' balances, I must design and fill in the related tables.

The Figure 1-5 shows the original proof of the first transaction, seeing the next page. First, the transaction sub-equation is:

Cash (1) = Share capital (3)

Because the "Cash" account is the first parent account of writing into 1 class accounts (X1) table and the "Share capital" account is also the first parent account of writing into 3 class accounts (X3) table, the transaction's mathematical sub-equation is:

$X101 = X301$

Second, the account of the X101 has a two-level subaccount and the account of the X301 has the three one-level subaccounts (seeing the Figure 1-5), so the one-level and the two-level expanding mathematical sub-equations are the following:

One-level sub-equation $X10101 = X30101 + X30102 + X30103$
Two-level sub-equation $X1010101 = X30101 + X30102 + X30103$

From the Figure 1-5, the X10101 is the "Financing activities" and the X1010101 is the "Cash receipts from owners"; the X30101, the X30102, and the X30103 are respectively the "Capital-Ping Wang", the "Capital-Hua Li", and the "Capital-Mike Newsome". In addition, the terms of the X1010101, the X30101, the X30102, and the X30103 in the above two-level sub-equation are the lowest subaccounts of their parent accounts in this transaction, so their amounts are $10,000, $4,000, $3,000, and $3,000 respectively.

Transaction Original Proof							
Transaction Date: 1/2/2016						General ID	1
Explanation: Ping Wang, Hua Li and Mike Newsome decide to open a RR trade business							
No.	Class	Account Name	Left Amount	Right Amount	MultiSubaccount Name	Subtotal Name	Ref
1	1	Cash	10000		Cash receipts from owners< Financing activities	Current assets,103	104
2	3	Share capital		4000	Capital-Ping Wang	Owners'capital,303	304
3	3	Share capital		3000	Capital-Hua Li		
4	3	Share capital		3000	Capital-Mike Newsome		
5							
6							
7							
8							
Total			10000	10000			
Customer or Supplier's Name			Address		E-mail		Postal Code
City			State		Country		

Person Handling: Manager:

Date: Date:

Figure 1-5   Original Proof of First Transaction

Third, when the two-level sub-equation is added to the one-level sub-equation, the amount of the upper subaccount X10101 is $10,000 (= X1010101) and the amounts of the X30101, X30102, and X30103 do not change. When the one-level sub-equation is added to the transaction sub-equation, the amount of the parent account X101 is $10,000 (= X10101) and the amount of the parent account X301 is $10,000 (= X30101 + X30102 + X30103).

Finally, for getting the balances of all related parent accounts and their subaccounts, I should create some tables: General equation, Class accounts, Parent accounts, and subaccounts. Then I fill in these tables with this transaction information and calculate their balances. The Table 1 shows the general equation, the Table 2 shows the class accounts of the assets accounts (X1) and the shareholders' equity accounts (X3), and the Table 3 shows the parent accounts of the "Cash (X101)" and the "Share capital (X301)". The Table 4 shows the one-level subaccounts of the "Financing activities (X10101)", the "Capital-Ping Wang (X30101)", the "Capital-Hua Li (X30102)", and the "Capital-Mike Newsome (X30103)". The Table 5 shows the two-level subaccount of the "Cash receipts from owners (X1010101)", seeing the following tables.

Table 1 General equation

GeID	Transaction Date	General Equation	Left Amount	Right Amount	Explanation	Enter Date
1	2014-1-2	Cash(1): 10000 = Share capital(3): 4000 + Share capital(3): 3000 + Share capital(3): 3000	10000	10000	Ping Wang, Hua Li and Mike Newsome decide to open a RR trade business	2015-2-8
Total Amount			**10000**	**10000**		

Table 2 Class Accounts

Assets (X1)

ID	Account Name (Mathematical Name)	Subtotal	Ref (Row)	Balance
1	Cash (X101)	Current assets,103	104	10000

Shareholders' Equity (X3)

ID	Account Name (Mathematical Name)	Subtotal	Ref (Row)	Balance
1	Share capital (X301)	Owners' Capital,303	304	10000

Table 3 Parent Accounts

Cash (X101)

ID	MultiName	Amount	Ref	Balance	GeID	SubFirst	SubSecond	SubThird	Unit
1	Cash receipts from owners<Financing activities	10000		10000	1	Financing activities	Cash receipts from owners		1

Share capital (X301)

ID	MultiName	Amount	Ref	Balance	GeID	SubFirst	SubSecond	SubThird	Unit
1	Capital-Ping Wang	4000		4000	1	Capital-Ping Wang			1
2	Capital-Hua Li	3000		7000	1	Capital-Hua Li			1
3	Capital-Mike Newsome	3000		10000	1	Capital-Mike Newsome			1

Table 4 One-level subaccounts

Financing activities (X10101) < Parent account: Cash (X101)

ID	MultiName	Amount	Ref	GeID	Transaction Date	Balance
1	Cash receipts from owners<Financing activities	10000		1	2014-1-2	10000

Capital-Ping Wang (X30101) < Parent account: Share capital (X301)

ID	MultiName	Amount	Ref	GeID	Transaction Date	Balance
1	Capital-Ping Wang	4000		1	2014-1-2	4000

Capital- Hua Li (X30102) < Parent account: Share capital (X301)

ID	MultiName	Amount	Ref	GeID	Transaction Date	Balance
1	Capital-Hua Li	3000		1	2014-1-2	3000

Capital-Mike Newsome (X30103) < Parent account: Share capital (X301)

ID	MultiName	Amount	Ref	GeID	Transaction Date	Balance
1	Capital- Mike Newsome	3000		1	2014-1-2	3000

Table 5 Two-level subaccount

Cash receipts from owners (X1010101) << Parent account: Cash (X101)

ID	MultiName	Amount	Ref	GeID	Transaction Date	Balance
1	Cash receipts from owners<Financing activities	10000		1	2014-1-2	10000

I write the lowest subaccounts' amounts into their tables respectively and calculate their balances. The table "Cash receipts from owners (X1010101)" in the Table 5 is the lowest subaccount (two-level subaccount) of the parent account "Cash(X101)", so I write the $10,000 into this table in the Table 5. The three tables of the "Capital-Ping Wang(X30101)", the "Capital-Hua Li(X30102)" , and the "Capital-Mike Newsome(X30103)" in the Table 4 are the lowest subaccounts (one-level subaccounts) of the parent account "Share capital(X301)", so I respectively write the $4,000, $3,000, and $3,000 into the three tables in the Table 4.

Another table "Financing activities (X10101)" in the Table 4 can be gotten from the table "Cash receipts from owners (X1010101)" in the Table 5. The accounts of the "Cash(X101)" and the "Share capital(X301)" parent accounts in the Table 3 can be respectively gotten from the table of the "Financing activities (X10101)" and the tables of the "Capital-Ping Wang (X30101)", the "Capital- Hua Li (X30102)", and the "Capital-Mike Newsome (X30103)" in the Table 4.

The two tables' balances in the Table 2 can be gotten from the two tables of the "Cash (X101)" and the "Share capital (X301) in the Table 3 respectively.

In fact, database can do the work easily by using of the MathAccounting software. After entering the transaction, the database has created two tables of the "Cash (X101)" and the "Share capital (X301)" parent accounts, and calculated their balances. Meanwhile, the tables of all subaccounts (including one-level subaccounts of the "Financing activities (X10101)", the "Capital-Ping Wang (X30101)", the "Capital-Hua Li (X30102)", and the "Capital-Mike Newsome (X30103)" and the two-level subaccount of the "Cash receipts from owners (X1010101)"), and their balances can be gotten by using of the database query.

The Figure 1-6 shows the original proof of second transaction, seeing the next page.

Transaction Original Proof							
Transaction Date: 1/3/2016						General ID	2
Explanation: Purchase of supplies							
No.	Class	Account Name	Left Amount	Right Amount	MultiSubaccount Name	Subtotal Name	Ref
1	1	Cash	-193		Cash payments for operating expenses< Operating activities		
2	1	Supplies	193		N	Current assets,103	106
3							
4							
5							
6							
7							
8							
Total			0	0			
Customer or Supplier's Name			Address		E-mail	Postal Code	
City			State		Country		

Person Handling: Manager:

Date: Date:

Figure 1-6   Original Proof of Second Transaction

The transaction sub-equation is:

Cash (1) + Supplies (1) = 0

Because the "Supplies" is the second parent account of writing into 1 class accounts (X1) table, the transaction's mathematical sub-equation is:

$X101 + X102 = 0$

The account of the X101 has a different two-level subaccount (whose one-level subaccount is also different from the first transaction) and the account of the X102 has not any subaccount (seeing the Figure 1-6), so the one-level and the two-level expanding mathematical sub-equations are the following:

One-level sub-equation   X10102 + X102 = 0

Two-level sub-equation   X1010201 + X102 = 0

From the Figure 1-6, the X10102 is the "Operating activities" and the X1010201 is the "Cash payments for operating expenses". The amounts of the X1010201 and the X102 in the two-level sub-equation are respectively -$193 and $193.

When the two-level sub-equation is added to the one-level sub-equation, the amount of the upper subaccount X10102 is -$193 (= X1010201) and the amount of the parent account X102 does not change. When the one-level sub-equation is added to the transaction sub-equation, the amount of the parent account X101 is -$193 (= X10102) and the amount of the parent account X102 is $193 (= X102).

For recording the transaction, I should create three tables of the parent account "Supplies (X102)", one-level subaccount "Operating activities (X10102)", and the two-level subaccount "Cash payments for operating expenses (X1010201)", and calculate their balances. The two tables of the general equation and the parent account "Cash (X101)" have existed, so I should only update their information.

The Table 6 shows the general equation, the Table 7 shows the class accounts of the assets accounts (X1), the Table 8 shows the parent accounts of the "Cash (X101)" and "Supplies (X102)", the Table 9 shows the one-level subaccount "Operating activities (X10102)", and the Table 10 shows the two-level subaccount "Cash payments for operating expenses (X1010201)", seeing the following tables.

Table 6 General equation

GeID	Transaction Date	General Equation	Left Amount	Right Amount	Explanation	Enter Date
1	2016-1-2	Cash(1): 10000 = Share capital(3): 4000 + Capital(3): 3000 + Capital(3): 3000	10000	10000	Ping Wang, Hua Li and Mike Newsome decide to open a RR trade business	2016-2-8
2	2016-1-3	Cash(1): -193 + Supplies(1): 193 = 0	0	0	Purchase of supplies	2016-2-8
Total Amount			**10000**	**10000**		

Table 7 Class Accounts

Assets (X1)

ID	Account Name (Mathematical Name)	Subtotal	Ref (Row)	Balance
1	Cash (X101)	Current assets,103	104	9807
2	Supplies (X102)	Current assets,103	106	193

Table 8 Parent accounts

Cash (X101)

ID	MultiName	Amount	Ref	Balance	GeID	SubFirst	SubSecond	SubThird	Unit
1	Cash receipts from owners<Financing activities	10000		10000	1	Financing activities	Cash receipts from owners		1
2	Cash payments for operating expenses<Operating activities	-193		9807	2	Operating activities	Cash payments for operating expenses		1

Supplies (X102)

ID	MultiName	Amount	Ref	Balance	GeID	SubFirst	SubSecond	SubThird	Unit
1	n	193		193	2				1

Table 9 One-level subaccount

Operating activities (X10102) < Parent account: Cash (X101)

ID	MultiName	Amount	Ref	GeID	Transaction Date	Balance
1	Cash payments for operating expenses<Operating activities	-193		2	2014-1-3	-193

Table 10 Two-level subaccount

Cash payments for operating expenses (X1010201) << Parent account: Cash (X101)

ID	MultiName	Amount	Ref	GeID	Transaction Date	Balance
1	Cash payments for operating expenses<Operating activities	-193		2	2014-1-3	-193

I write the lowest subaccounts' amounts into their tables respectively and calculate their balances. The table "Cash payments for operating expenses (X1010201)" in the Table 10 is the lowest subaccount (two-level subaccount) of the parent account "Cash (X101)", so I write the -$193 into this table in the Table 10. Because the parent account "Supplies (X102)" has not any subaccount, I write the $193 into the parent account table "Supplies (X102)" in the Table 8.

The table "Operating activities (X10102)" in the Table 9 can be gotten from the table "Cash payments for operating expenses(X1010201)" in the Table 10.

The parent account of the "Cash (X101)" in the Table 8 can be gotten from the table of the "Operating activities(X10102)" in the Table 9.

The balances of the table "Assets (X1)" in the Table 7 can be gotten from the tables of the "Cash (X101)" and the "Supplies (X102)" in the Table 8.

The Figure 1-7 on the next page shows the original proof of third transaction. The transaction sub-equation is:

Cash (1) = Travelling expenses (5)

Because the "Travelling expenses" is the first parent account of writing into 5 class accounts (X5) table, the transaction's mathematical sub-equation is:

X101 = X501

The accounts of the X101 and X501 have the two-level subaccounts (seeing the Figure 1-7), so the one-level and the two-level expanding mathematical sub-equations are the following:

One-level sub-equation   X10102 = X50101
Two-level sub-equation   X1010201 = X5010101

From the Figure 1-7, the X10102 is the "Operating activities" and X1010201 is the "Cash payments for operating expenses"; the X50101 is the "Purchase department-travelling" and X5010101 is the "Hua Li-travelling".

\multicolumn{8}{c}{**Transaction Original Proof**}

Transaction Date: 1/3/2016						General ID	3
Explanation: Cash payment for Hua Li's taxi fee expense							
No.	Class	Account Name	Left Amount	Right Amount	MultiSubaccount Name	Subtotal Name	Ref
1	1	Cash	-47		Cash payments for operating expenses< Operating activities		
2	5	Travelling expenses		-47	909876507-travelling< Purchase department-travelling	Operating and administrative expenses,453	454
3							
4							
5							
6							
7							
8							
Total			-47	-47			
Customer or Supplier's Name		Address		E-mail		Postal Code	
City		State		Country			

Person Handling: Manager:

Date: Date:

Figure 1-7   Original Proof of Third Transaction

The same method can be used to calculate the amounts of the parent accounts and their subaccounts.

For recording the transaction, I should create three tables of the parent account "Travelling expenses (X501)", the one-level subaccount "Purchase department-travelling (X50101)", and the two-level subaccount "Hua Li-travelling (X5010101)", and calculate their balances. The tables of the parent account "Cash (X101)", the one-level subaccount "Operating activities (X10102)", and the two-level subaccount "Cash payments for operating expenses (X10102001)" have existed, so I should only update their information.

The Table 11 shows the general equation, the Table 12 shows the class accounts of the assets accounts (X1) and the expenses accounts (X5), the Table 13 shows the parent accounts of the "Cash (X101)" and "Travelling expenses (X501)", the Table 14 shows the one-level subaccounts of the "Operating activities (X10102)" and the "Purchase department-travelling (X50101)", and the Table 15 shows the two-level subaccounts of the "Cash payments for operating expenses (X1010201)" and the "Hua Li-travelling (X5010101)", seeing the following tables.

Table 11 General equation

GeID	Transaction Date	General Equation	Left Amount	Right Amount	Explanation	Enter Date
1	2014-1-2	Cash(1): 10000 = Share capital(3): 4000 + Capital(3): 3000 + Capital(3): 3000	10000	10000	Ping Wang, Hua Li and Mike Newsome decide to open a RR trade business	2015-2-8
2	2014-1-3	Cash(1): -193 + Supplies(1): 193 = 0	0	0	Purchase of supplies	2015-2-8
3	2014-1-3	Cash(1): -47 = Expenses (5): -47	-47	-47	Cash payments for Hua Li's taxi fee expense	2015-2-8
Total Amount			**9953**	**9953**		

Table 12 Class accounts

Assets (X1)

ID	Account Name (Mathematical Name)	Subtotal	Ref (Row)	Balance
1	Cash (X101)	Current assets,103	104	9760
2	Supplies (X102)	Current assets,103	106	193

Expenses (X5)

ID	Account Name (Mathematical Name)	Subtotal	Ref (Row)	Balance
1	Travelling expenses (X501)	Operating and administrative expenses,453	454	-47

Table 13 Parent accounts

Cash (X101)

ID	MultiName	Amount	Ref	Balance	GeID	SubFirst	SubSecond	SubThird	Unit
1	Cash receipts from owners<Financing activities	10000		10000	1	Financing activities	Cash receipts from owners		1
2	Cash payments for operating expenses<Operating activities	-193		9807	2	Operating activities	Cash payments for operating expenses		1
3	Cash payments for operating expenses<Operating activities	-47		9760	3	Operating activities	Cash payments for operating expenses		1

Travelling expenses (X501)

ID	MultiName	Amount	Ref	Balance	GeID	SubFirst	SubSecond	SubThird	Unit
1	Hua Li-travelling< Purchase department-travelling	-47		-47	3	Purchase Department-travelling	Hua Li-travelling		1

Table 14 One-level subaccounts

Operating activities (X10102) < Parent account: Cash (X101)

ID	MultiName	Amount	Ref	GeID	Transaction Date	Balance
1	Cash payments for operating expenses<Operating activities	-193		2	2014-1-3	-193
2	Cash payments for operating expenses<Operating activities	-47		3	2014-1-3	-240

Purchase Department-travelling (X50101) < Parent account: Travelling expenses (X501)

ID	MultiName	Amount	Ref	GeID	Transaction Date	Balance
1	Hua Li-travelling< Purchase department-travelling	-47		3	2014-1-5	-47

Table 15 Two-level subaccounts

Cash payments for operating expenses (X1010201) << Parent account: Cash (X101)

ID	MultiName	Amount	Ref	GeID	Transaction Date	Balance
1	Cash payments for operating expenses<Operating activities	-193		2	2014-1-3	-193
2	Cash payments for operating expenses<Operating activities	-47		3	2014-1-3	-240

Hua Li-travelling (X5010101) << Parent account: Travelling expenses (X501)

ID	MultiName	Amount	Ref	GeID	Transaction Date	Balance
1	Hua Li-travelling< Purchase department-travelling	-47		3	2014-1-5	-47

I write the lowest subaccounts' amounts into their tables respectively and calculate their balances. The two tables of the "Cash payments for operating expenses (X1010201)" and

"Hua Li-travelling (X5010101)" in the Table 15 are the lowest subaccounts (two-level subaccounts) of the parent accounts of the "Cash(X101)" and "Travelling expenses (X501)" respectively, so I write the -$47 into the two tables in the Table 15 respectively.

The two tables of the "Operating activities (X10102)" and "Purchase department-travelling (X50101)" in the Table 14 can be gotten from the two tables of the "Cash payments for operating expenses (X1010201)" and the "Hua Li-travelling (X5010101)" in the Table 15 respectively.

The two tables of the parent accounts of the "Cash (X101)" and the "Travelling expenses (X501)" in the Table 13 can be gotten from the two tables of the "Operating activities (X10102)" and the "Purchase department-travelling (X50101)" in the Table 14 respectively.

The balances of the tables of the "Assets (X1)" and the "Expenses (X5)" in the Table 12 can be gotten from the two tables of the "Cash (X101)" and the "Travelling expenses (X501)" in the Table 13 respectively.

The Figure 1-8 on the next page shows the original proof of fourth transaction. The transaction sub-equation is:

Cash (1) + Inventory (1) = Account payable (2)

Because the "Inventory" is the third parent account of writing into 1 class accounts (X1) table and the "Account payable" is the first parent account of writing into 2 class accounts (X2) table, the transaction's mathematical sub-equation is:

$X101 + X103 = X201$

The account of the X101 has a different two-level subaccount (seeing the Figure 1-8), the account of the X103 has the three-level subaccounts, and the account of the X201 has a one-level subaccount, so the one-level, the two-level, and the three-level expanding mathematical sub-equations are the following:

One-level sub-equation $X10102 + X10301 = X20101$

Two-level sub-equation $X1010202 + X1030101 + X1030102 + X1030103 = X20101$

Three-level sub-equation $X1010202 + X103010101 + X103010102 + X103010201 +$

$$X103010202 + X1030103 = X20101$$

Transaction Original Proof

No.	Class	Account Name	Left Amount	Right Amount	MultiSubaccount Name	Subtotal Name	Ref

Transaction Date: 1/5/2016 — General ID: 4

Explanation: RR purchases $3,670 inventory by $670 cash and other on credit from A1 company (phone number: 987654321)

No.	Class	Account Name	Left Amount	Right Amount	MultiSubaccount Name	Subtotal Name	Ref
1	1	Cash	-670		Cash payments to suppliers< Operating activities		
2	1	Inventory	10*165		Inven111<Inven11<Inven1	Current assets,103	108
3	1	Inventory	4*225		Inven112<Inven11<Inven1		
4	1	Inventory	0.8*650		Inven121<Inven12<Inven1		
5	1	Inventory	5*66		Inven122<Inven12<Inven1		
6	1	Inventory	30*9		Inven13<Inven1		
7	2	Account payable		3000	987654321	Current liabilities,203	204
8							
Total			3000	3000			

Customer or Supplier's Name	Address	E-mail		Postal Code
A1	A2	A3		A4
City	State	Country		
A5	A6	A7		

Person Handling: Manager:

Date: Date:

Figure 1-8   Original Proof of Fourth Transaction

From the Figure 1-8, the X10102 is the "Operating activities" and the X1010202 is the "Cash payments to suppliers"; the X10301, the X1030101, the X1030102, the X1030103, the X103010101, the X103010102, the X103010201, and the X103010202 are respectively the "Inven1", the "Inven11", the "Inven12", the "Inven13", the "Inven111", the "Inven112", the "Inven121", and the "Inven122"; the X20101 is the "987654321".

The same method can be used to calculate the amounts of the parent accounts and their subaccounts.

For recording the transaction, I should create two tables of the parent accounts of the "Inventory (X103)" and "Account payable (X201)", and calculated their balances. Meanwhile, I should also create the tables of one-level subaccounts (including the "Inven1", the "Inven2", the "Inven3", and the "987654321"), two-level subaccounts (including the "Cash payments to suppliers", the "Inven11", the "Inven12", and the "Inven13"), and three-level subaccounts (including the "Inven111", the "Inven112", the "Inven121", and the "Inven122"). The table of the parent account "Cash (X101)" has existed, so I should only update its information, including its subaccounts' information.

The Table 16 shows the general equation. The Table 17 shows the class accounts of the assets accounts (X1) and the liabilities accounts (X2). The Table 18 shows the three parent accounts of the "Cash (X101)", the "Inventory (X103)", and the "Account payable (X201)". The Table 19 shows the three one-level subaccounts of the "Operating activities", the"Inven1", and the "987654321". The Table 20 shows the four two-level subaccounts of the "Cash payments to suppliers", the "Inven11", the "Inven12", and the "Inven13". The Table 21 shows the four three-level subaccounts of the "Inven111", the "Inven112", the "Inven121", and the "Inven122", seeing the following tables.

In addition, I should also create a table to record the suppliers' information, seeing the Table 22 which is below the Table 21.

Table 16 General equation

GeID	Transaction Date	General Equation	Left Amount	Right Amount	Explanation	Enter Date
1	2016-1-2	Cash(1): 10000 = Share capital(3): 4000 + Capital(3): 3000 + Capital(3): 3000	10000	10000	Ping Wang, Hua Li and Mike Newsome decide to open a RR trade business	2016-2-8
2	2016-1-3	Cash(1): -193 + Supplies(1): 193 = 0	0	0	Purchase of supplies	2016-2-8
3	2016-1-3	Cash(1): -47 = Expenses (5): -47	-47	-47	Cash payments for Hua Li's taxi fee expense	2016-2-8
4	2016-1-5	Cash(1): -670 +Inventory(1): 3670 = Account payable(2): 3000	3000	3000	RR purchases $3,670 inventory by $670 cash and other on credit from A1 company (phone number: 987654321)	2016-2-8
Total Amount			12953	12953		

Table 17 Class accounts

Assets (X1)

ID	Account Name (Mathematical Name)	Subtotal	Ref (Row)	Balance
1	Cash (X101)	Current assets,103	104	9090
2	Supplies (X102)	Current assets,103	106	193
3	Inventory (X103)	Current assets,103	108	3670

Liabilities (X2)

ID	Account Name (Mathematical Name)	Subtotal	Ref (Row)	Balance
1	Account payable (X201)	Current liabilities,203	204	3000

Table 18 Parent accounts

Cash (X101)

ID	MultiName	Amount	Ref	Balance	GeID	SubFirst	SubSecond	SubThird	Unit
1	Cash receipts from owners<Financing activities	10000		10000	1	Financing activities	Cash receipts from owners		1
2	Cash payments for operating expenses<Operating activities	-193		9807	2	Operating activities	Cash payments for operating expenses		1
3	Cash payments for operating expenses<Operating activities	-47		9760	3	Operating activities	Cash payments for operating expenses		1
4	Cash payments to suppliers< Operating activities	-670		9090	4	Operating activities	Cash payments to suppliers		1

Inventory (X103)

ID	MultiName	Amount	Ref	Balance	GeID	SubFirst	SubSecond	SubThird	Unit
1	Inven111<Inven11< Inven1	10*165		1650	4	Inven1	Inven11	Inven111	165
2	Inven112<Inven11< Inven1	4*225		2550	4	Inven1	Inven11	Inven112	225
3	Inven121<Inven12< Inven1	0.8*650		3070	4	Inven1	Inven12	Inven121	650
4	Inven122<Inven12< Inven1	5*66		3400	4	Inven1	Inven12	Inven122	66
5	Inven13<Inven1	30*9		3670	4	Inven1	Inven13		9

Account payable (X201)

ID	MultiName	Amount	Ref	Balance	GeID	SubFirst	SubSecond	SubThird	Unit
1	987654321	3000		3000	4	987654321			1

Table 19 One-level subaccounts

Operating activities (X10102) < Parent account: Cash (X101)

ID	MultiName	Amount	Ref	GeID	Transaction Date	Balance
1	Cash payments for operating expenses<Operating activities	-193		2	2014-1-3	-193
2	Cash payments for operating expenses<Operating activities	-47		3	2014-1-3	-240
3	Cash payments to suppliers< Operating activities	-670		4	2014-1-5	-910

Inven1 (X10301) < Parent account: Inventory (X103)

ID	MultiName	Amount	Ref	GeID	Transaction Date	Balance
1	Inven111<Inven11<Inven1	10*165		4	2014-1-5	1650
2	Inven112<Inven11<Inven1	4*225		4	2014-1-5	2550
3	Inven121<Inven12<Inven1	0.8*650		4	2014-1-5	3070
4	Inven122<Inven12<Inven1	5*66		4	2014-1-5	3400
5	Inven13<Inven1	30*9		4	2014-1-5	3670

987654321 (X20101) < Parent account: Account payable (X201)

ID	MultiName	Amount	Ref	GeID	Transaction Date	Balance
1	987654321	3000		4	2014-1-5	3000

Table 20 Two-level subaccounts

Cash payments to suppliers (X1010202) << Parent account: Cash (X101)

ID	MultiName	Amount	Ref	GeID	Transaction Date	Balance
1	Cash payments to suppliers< Operating activities	-670		4	2014-1-5	-670

Inven11 (X1030101) << Parent account: Inventory (X103)

ID	MultiName	Amount	Ref	GeID	Transaction Date	Balance
1	Inven111<Inven11<Inven1	10*165		4	2014-1-5	1650
2	Inven112<Inven11<Inven1	4*225		4	2014-1-5	2550

Inven12 (X1030102) << Parent account: Inventory (X103)

ID	MultiName	Amount	Ref	GeID	Transaction Date	Balance
1	Inven121<Inven12<Inven1	0.8*650		4	2014-1-5	520
2	Inven122<Inven12<Inven1	5*66		4	2014-1-5	850

Inven13 (X1030103) << Parent account: Inventory (X103)

ID	MultiName	Amount	Ref	GeID	Transaction Date	Balance
1	Inven13<Inven1	30*9		4	2014-1-5	270

Table 21 Three-level subaccounts

Inven111 (X103010101) <<< Parent account: Inventory (X103)

ID	MultiName	Amount	Ref	GeID	Transaction Date	Balance
1	Inven111<Inven11<Inven1	10*165		4	2014-1-5	1650

Inven112 (X103010102) <<< Parent account: Inventory (X103)

ID	MultiName	Amount	Ref	GeID	Transaction Date	Balance
1	Inven112<Inven11<Inven1	4*225		4	2014-1-5	900

Inven121 (X103010201) <<< Parent account: Inventory (X103)

ID	MultiName	Amount	Ref	GeID	Transaction Date	Balance
1	Inven121<Inven12<Inven1	0.8*650		4	2014-1-5	520

Inven122 (X103010202) <<< Parent account: Inventory (X103)

ID	MultiName	Amount	Ref	GeID	Transaction Date	Balance
1	Inven122<Inven12<Inven1	5*66		4	2014-1-5	330

Table 22 Suppliers information

ID	Supplier Phone	Supplier Name	Address	E-mail	Postal Code	City	State	Country
1	987654321	A1	A2	A3	A4	A5	A6	A7

I write the lowest subaccounts' amounts into their tables respectively and calculate their balances. The four tables of the "Inven111 (X103010101)", the "Inven112 (X103010102)", the "Inven121 (X103010201)", and the "Inven122 (X103010202)" in the Table 21 are the lowest subaccounts (three-level subaccounts) of the parent account of the "Inventory (X103)" respectively, so I write the $10*165, $4*225, $0.8*650, and $5*66 into the four tables in the Table 21 respectively. The two tables of the "Cash payments to suppliers (X1010202)" and the "Inven13 (X1030103)" in the Table 20 are the lowest subaccounts (two-level subaccounts) of the parent accounts of the "Cash (X101)" and the "Inventory (X103)" respectively, so I write -$670 and $30*9 into the two tables in Table 20 respectively. The table of the "987654321 (X20101)" in the Table 19 is the lowest subaccount (one-level subaccount) of the parent account "Account payable (X201)", so I write $3000 into this table in the Table 19. In addition, I also write the supplier's information into the Table 22 which is below the Table 21.

The two tables of the "Inven11 (X1030101)" and the "Inven12 (X1030102)" in the Table 20 can be gotten from the four tables of the "Inven111 (X103010101)", the "Inven112 (X103010102)", the "Inven121 (X103010201)", and the "Inven122 (X103010202)" in the Table 21 respectively.

The two tables of the "Operating activities (X10102)" and the "Inven1 (X10301)" in the Table 19 can be gotten from the four tables of the "Cash payments to suppliers (X1010202)", the "Inven11 (X1030101)", the "Inven12 (X1030102)", and the "Inven13 (X1030103)" in the Table 20 respectively.

The three tables of the parent accounts of the "Cash(X101)", the "Inventory (X103)", and the "Account payable (X201)" in the Table 18 can be gotten from the three tables of the one-level subaccounts of the "Operating activities (X10102)", the "Inven1 (X10301)", and the "987654321 (X20101)" in the Table 19 respectively.

The balances of the tables of the "Assets (X1)" and the "Liabilities (X2)" in the Table 17 can be gotten from the three tables of the "Cash (X101)", the "Inventory (X103)", and the "Account payable (X201)" in the Table 18 respectively.

The Figure 1-9 on the next page shows the original proof of fifth transaction. The transaction sub-equation is:

Cash (1) + Inventory (1) +Account receivable (1) = Sales (4) + Cost of sales (5)

Because the "Account receivable" is the fourth parent account of writing into 1 class accounts (X1) table, the "Sales" is the first parent account of writing into 4 class accounts (X4) table, and the "Cost of sales" is the second parent account of writing into 5 class accounts (X5) table, so the transaction's mathematical sub-equation is:

X101 + X103 + X104 = X401 + X502

<table>
<tr><td colspan="8" align="center">Transaction Original Proof</td></tr>
<tr><td colspan="6">Transaction Date: 1/5/2016</td><td>General ID</td><td>5</td></tr>
<tr><td colspan="8">Explanation: RR sells $1,900 inventory to B1 Company (phone number: 123456789) for sales of $2,530 and receives $300 cash</td></tr>
<tr><td>No.</td><td>Class</td><td>Account Name</td><td>Left Amount</td><td>Right Amount</td><td>MultiSubaccount Name</td><td>Subtotal Name</td><td>Ref</td></tr>
<tr><td>1</td><td>1</td><td>Cash</td><td>300</td><td></td><td>Cash receipts from customers< Operating activities</td><td></td><td></td></tr>
<tr><td>2</td><td>1</td><td>Inventory</td><td>-10*91</td><td></td><td>Inven111<Inven11<Inven1</td><td></td><td></td></tr>
<tr><td>3</td><td>1</td><td>Inventory</td><td>-4*130</td><td></td><td>Inven112<Inven11<Inven1</td><td></td><td></td></tr>
<tr><td>4</td><td>1</td><td>Inventory</td><td>-0.8*375</td><td></td><td>Inven121<Inven12<Inven1</td><td></td><td></td></tr>
<tr><td>5</td><td>1</td><td>Inventory</td><td>-5*34</td><td></td><td>Inven122<Inven12<Inven1</td><td></td><td></td></tr>
<tr><td>6</td><td>1</td><td>Account receivable</td><td>2230</td><td></td><td>123456789</td><td>Current assets,103</td><td>110</td></tr>
<tr><td>7</td><td>4</td><td>Sales</td><td></td><td>2530</td><td>909876511-sales</td><td>Revenues,403</td><td>404</td></tr>
<tr><td>8</td><td>5</td><td>Cost of sales</td><td></td><td>-1900</td><td>N</td><td>Cost,431</td><td>432</td></tr>
<tr><td colspan="3">Total</td><td>630</td><td>630</td><td></td><td></td><td></td></tr>
<tr><td colspan="3" align="center">Customer or Supplier's Name</td><td>Address</td><td colspan="2" align="center">E-mail</td><td colspan="2" align="center">Postal Code</td></tr>
<tr><td colspan="3" align="center">B1</td><td>B2</td><td colspan="2" align="center">B3</td><td colspan="2" align="center">B4</td></tr>
<tr><td colspan="3" align="center">City</td><td>State</td><td colspan="2" align="center">Country</td><td colspan="2"></td></tr>
<tr><td colspan="3" align="center">B5</td><td>B6</td><td colspan="2" align="center">B7</td><td colspan="2"></td></tr>
</table>

Person Handling: Manager:

Date: Date:

Figure 1-9   Original Proof of Fifth Transaction

The account of the X101 has a different two-level subaccount, the account of the X103 has the three-level subaccounts, the accounts of the X104 and X401 have the one-level subaccounts, and the account of the X502 has not any subaccount (seeing the Figure 9), so the one-level, the two-level and three-level expanding mathematical sub-equations are the following:

One-level sub-equation $X10102 + X10301 + X10401 = X40101 + X502$

Two-level sub-equation $X1010203 + X1030101 + X1030102 + X10401 = X40101 + X502$

Three-level sub-equation $X1010203 + X103010101 + X103010102 + X103010201 +$
$$X103010202 + X10401 = X40101 + X502$$

From the Figure 1-9, the X10102 is the "Operating activities" and the X1010203 is the "Cash receipts from customers"; the X10301, the X1030101, the X1030102, the X103010101, the X103010102, the X103010201, and the X103010202 are respectively the "Inven1", the "Inven11", the "Inven12", the "Inven111", the "Inven112", the "Inven121", and the "Inven122"; the X10401 is the "123456789"; the X40101 is the "Xiao Zhou-sales".

The same method can be used to calculate the amounts of the parent accounts and their subaccounts.

For recording the transaction, I should create three tables of the parent accounts of the "Account receivable", the "Sales", and the "Account payable", and calculated their balances. Meanwhile, I should also create two tables of the one-level subaccounts of the "987654321" and the "Xiao Zhou-sales". The tables of the parent accounts of the "Cash" and the "Inventory" have existed, so I should only update their information, including their subaccounts' information.

The Table 23 shows the general equation. The Table 24 shows the class accounts of the assets accounts (X1), the revenues accounts (X4), and the expenses accounts (X5). The Table 25 shows the parent accounts of the "Cash", the "Account receivable", the "Sales", and the "Cost of sales". The Table 26 shows the one-level subaccounts (including the "Operating activities", the "Inven1", the "123456789", and the "Xiao Zhou-sales), the Table 27 shows the two-level subaccounts (including the "Cash receipts from customers", the "Inven11", the "Inven12", and the "Inven13"), and the Table 28 shows the three-level subaccounts (including the "Inven111", the "Inven112", the "Inven121", and the "Inven122"), seeing the following tables.

In addition, I should also create a table to record the customers' information, seeing the Table 29 which is below the Table 28.

Table 23 General equation

GeID	Transaction Date	General Equation	Left Amount	Right Amount	Explanation	Enter Date
1	2016-1-2	Cash(1): 10000 = Share capital(3): 4000 + Capital(3): 3000 + Capital(3): 3000	10000	10000	Ping Wang, Hua Li and Mike Newsome decide to open a RR trade business	2016-2-8
2	2016-1-3	Cash(1): -193 + Supplies(1): 193 = 0	0	0	Purchase of supplies	2016-2-8
3	2016-1-3	Cash(1): -47 = Expenses (5): -47	-47	-47	Cash payments for Hua Li's taxi fee expense	2016-2-8
4	2016-1-5	Cash(1): -670 +Inventory(1): 3670 = Account payable(2): 3000	3000	3000	RR purchases $3,670 inventory by $670 cash and other on credit from A1 company (phone number: 987654321)	2016-2-8
5	2016-1-5	Cash(1): 300 + Inventory(1): -1900 + Account receivable: 2230 = Revenues(4): 2530 + Expenses(5): -1900	630	630	RR sells $1,900 inventory to B1 Company (phone number: 123456789) for sales of $2,530 and receives $300 cash	2016-2-8
Total Amount			**13583**	**13583**		

Table 24 Class accounts

Assets (X1)

ID	Account Name (Mathematical Name)	Subtotal	Ref (Row)	Balance
1	Cash (X101)	Current assets,103	104	9390
2	Supplies (X102)	Current assets,103	106	193
3	Inventory (X103)	Current assets,103	108	1770
4	Account receivable (X104)	Current assets,103	110	2230

Revenues (X4)

ID	Account Name (Mathematical Name)	Subtotal	Ref (Row)	Balance
1	Sales (X401)	Revenues,403	404	2530

Expenses (X5)

ID	Account Name (Mathematical Name)	Subtotal	Ref (Row)	Balance
1	Travelling expenses (X501)	Operating and administrative expenses,453	454	-47
2	Cost of sales (X502)	Cost,431	432	-1900

Table 25 Parent accounts

Cash (X101)

ID	MultiName	Amount	Ref	Balance	GeID	SubFirst	SubSecond	SubThird	Unit
1	Cash receipts from owners<Financing activities	10000		10000	1	Financing activities	Cash receipts from owners		1
2	Cash payments for operating expenses<Operating activities	-193		9807	2	Operating activities	Cash payments for operating expenses		1
3	Cash payments for operating expenses<Operating activities	-47		9760	3	Operating activities	Cash payments for operating expenses		1
4	Cash payments to suppliers< Operating activities	-670		9090	4	Operating activities	Cash payments to suppliers		1
5	Cash receipts from customers< Operating activities	300		9390	5	Operating activities	Cash receipts from customers		1

Inventory (X103)

ID	MultiName	Amount	Ref	Balance	GeID	SubFirst	SubSecond	SubThird	Unit
1	Inven111<Inven11<Inven1	10*165		1650	4	Inven1	Inven11	Inven111	165
2	Inven112<Inven11<Inven1	4*225		2550	4	Inven1	Inven11	Inven112	225
3	Inven121<Inven12<Inven1	0.8*650		3070	4	Inven1	Inven12	Inven121	650
4	Inven122<Inven12<Inven1	5*66		3400	4	Inven1	Inven12	Inven122	66
5	Inven13<Inven1	30*9		3670	4	Inven1	Inven13		9
6	Inven111<Inven11<Inven1	-10*91		2760	5	Inven1	Inven11	Inven111	-91
7	Inven112<Inven11<Inven1	-4*130		2240	5	Inven1	Inven11	Inven112	-130
8	Inven121<Inven12<Inven1	-0.8*375		1940	5	Inven1	Inven12	Inven121	-375
9	Inven122<Inven12<Inven1	-5*34		1770	5	Inven1	Inven12	Inven122	-34

Account receivable (X104)

ID	MultiName	Amount	Ref	Balance	GeID	SubFirst	SubSecond	SubThird	Unit
1	123456789	2230		2230	5	123456789			1

Sales (X401)

ID	MultiName	Amount	Ref	Balance	GeID	SubFirst	SubSecond	SubThird	Unit
1	Xiao Zhou-sales	2530		2530	5	Xiao Zhou-sales			1

Cost of sales (X502)

ID	MultiName	Amount	Ref	Balance	GeID	SubFirst	SubSecond	SubThird	Unit
1	n	-1900		-1900	5				1

Table 26 One-level subaccounts

Operating activities (X10102) < Parent account: Cash (X101)

ID	MultiName	Amount	Ref	GeID	Transaction Date	Balance
1	Cash payments for operating expenses<Operating activities	-193		2	2014-1-3	-193
2	Cash payments for operating expenses<Operating activities	-47		3	2014-1-3	-240
3	Cash payments to suppliers< Operating activities	-670		4	2014-1-5	-910
4	Cash receipts from customers< Operating activities	300		5	2014-1-5	-610

Inven1 (X10301) < Parent account: Inventory (X103)

ID	MultiName	Amount	Ref	GeID	Transaction Date	Balance
1	Inven111<Inven11<Inven1	10*165		4	2014-1-5	1650
2	Inven112<Inven11<Inven1	4*225		4	2014-1-5	2550
3	Inven121<Inven12<Inven1	0.8*650		4	2014-1-5	3070
4	Inven122<Inven12<Inven1	5*66		4	2014-1-5	3400
5	Inven13<Inven1	30*9		4	2014-1-5	3670
6	Inven111<Inven11<Inven1	-10*91		5	2014-1-5	2760
7	Inven112<Inven11<Inven1	-4*130		5	2014-1-5	2240
8	Inven121<Inven12<Inven1	-0.8*375		5	2014-1-5	1940
9	Inven122<Inven12<Inven1	-5*34		5	2014-1-5	1770

123456789 (X10401) < Parent account: Account receivable (X104)

ID	MultiName	Amount	Ref	GeID	Transaction Date	Balance
1	123456789	2230		5	2014-1-5	2230

Xiao Zhou-sales (X40101) < Parent account: Sales (X401)

ID	MultiName	Amount	Ref	GeID	Transaction Date	Balance
1	Xiao Zhou-sales	2530		5	2014-1-5	2530

Table 27 Two-level subaccounts

Cash receipts from customers (X1010203) << Parent account: Cash (X101)

ID	MultiName	Amount	Ref	GeID	Transaction Date	Balance
1	Cash receipts from customers< Operating activities	300		5	2014-1-5	300

Inven11 (X1030101) << Parent account: Inventory (X103)

ID	MultiName	Amount	Ref	GeID	Transaction Date	Balance
1	Inven111<Inven11<Inven1	10*165		4	2014-1-5	1650
2	Inven112<Inven11<Inven1	4*225		4	2014-1-5	2550
3	Inven111<Inven11<Inven1	-10*91		5	2014-1-5	1640
4	Inven112<Inven11<Inven1	-4*130		5	2014-1-5	1120

Inven12 (X1030102) << Parent account: Inventory (X103)

ID	MultiName	Amount	Ref	GeID	Transaction Date	Balance
1	Inven121<Inven12<Inven1	0.8*650		4	2014-1-5	520
2	Inven122<Inven12<Inven1	5*66		4	2014-1-5	850
3	Inven121<Inven12<Inven1	-0.8*375		5	2014-1-5	550
4	Inven122<Inven12<Inven1	-5*34		5	2014-1-5	380

Table 28 Three-level subaccount

Inven111 (X103010101) <<< Parent account: Inventory (X103)

ID	MultiName	Amount	Ref	GeID	Transaction Date	Balance
1	Inven111<Inven11<Inven1	10*165		4	2014-1-5	1650
2	Inven111<Inven11<Inven1	-10*91		5	2014-1-5	740

Inven112 (X103010102) <<< Parent account: Inventory (X103)

ID	MultiName	Amount	Ref	GeID	Transaction Date	Balance
1	Inven112<Inven11<Inven1	4*225		4	2014-1-5	900
2	Inven112<Inven11<Inven1	-4*130		5	2014-1-5	380

Inven121 (X103010201) <<< Parent account: Inventory (X103)

ID	MultiName	Amount	Ref	GeID	Transaction Date	Balance
1	Inven121<Inven12<Inven1	0.8*650		4	2014-1-5	520
2	Inven121<Inven12<Inven1	-0.8*375		5	2014-1-5	220

Inven122 (X103010202) <<< Parent account: Inventory (X103)

ID	MultiName	Amount	Ref	GeID	Transaction Date	Balance
1	Inven122<Inven12<Inven1	5*66		4	2014-1-5	330
2	Inven122<Inven12<Inven1	-5*34		5	2014-1-5	160

Table 29 Customers information

ID	Customer Phone	Customer Name	Address	E-mail	Postal Code	City	State	Country
1	123456789	B1	B2	B3	B4	B5	B6	B7

I write the lowest subaccounts' amounts into their tables respectively and calculate their balances. The four tables of the "Inven111 (X103010101)", the "Inven112 (X103010102)", the "Inven121 (X103010201)", and the "Inven122 (X103010202)" in the Table 28 are the lowest subaccounts (three-level subaccounts) of the parent account of the "Inventory (X103)" respectively, so I write the -$10*91, -$4*130, -$0.8*375, and -$5*34 into the four tables in the Table 28 respectively. The table of the "Cash receipts from customers (X1010203)" in the Table 27 are the lowest subaccount (two-level subaccount) of the parent account of the "Cash (X101)", so I write the $300 into the Table 27. The two tables of the "123456789 (X10401)" and the "Xiao Zhou-sales (X40101)" in the Table 26 are the lowest subaccounts (one-level subaccounts) of the parent accounts of the "Account receivable (X104)" and the "Sales (X401)" respectively, so I write the $2230 and the $2530 into the two tables in the

Table 26 respectively. The parent account of the "Cost of sales (X502)" has not any subaccount, so I write -$1900 into the table of the "Cost of sales (X502)" in the Table 25. In addition, I also write the customer's information into the Table 29 which is below the Table 28.

The two tables of the "Inven11 (X1030101)" and the "Inven12 (X1030102)" in the Table 27 can be gotten from the four tables of the "Inven111 (X103010101)", the "Inven112 (X103010102)", the "Inven121 (X103010201)", and the "Inven122 (X103010202)" in the Table 28 respectively.

The two tables of the "Operating activities (X10102)" and "Inven1 (X10301)" in the Table 26 can be gotten from the three tables of the "Cash receipts from customers (X1010203)", the "Inven11 (X1030101)", and the "Inven12 (X1030102)" in the Table 27respectively.

The four tables of the parent accounts of the "Cash (X101)", the "Inventory (X103)", the "Account receivable (X104)", and the "Sales (X401)" in the Table 25 can be gotten from the four tables of the one-level subaccounts of the "Operating activities(X10102)", the "Inven1 (X10301)", the "123456789 (X10401)", and the "Xiao Zhou-sales (X40101)" in the Table 26 respectively.

The balances of the three tables of the "Assets (X1)", the "Revenues (X4)", and the "Expenses (X5)" in the Table 24 can be gotten from the five tables of the parent accounts of the "Cash (X101)", the "Inventory (X103)", "Account receivable (X104)", the "Sales (X401)", and the "Cost of sales (X502)" in the Table 25 respectively.

On January 28, 2014, RR Company receives $1,500 cash from B1 Company (phone number: 123456789) with the General ID 5.

The Figure 1-10 on the next page shows the original proof of sixth transaction.

Here, you must pay attention for the sixth transaction. In fact, when I receive the $1,500 cash, I know that B1 Company pays the cash with a General ID of the related transaction. Therefore, I borrow the Reference box to write the General ID of the related transaction. This General ID can be gotten from the previous transaction original proofs and is the "5".

Transaction Original Proof

No.	Class	Account Name	Left Amount	Right Amount	MultiSubaccount Name	Subtotal Name	Ref
1	1	Cash	1500		Cash receipts from customers< Operating activities		
2	1	Account receivable	-1500		123456789		**5**
3							
4							
5							
6							
7							
8							
Total			0	0			

Transaction Original Proof

Transaction Date: 1/28/2016 — General ID — 6

Explanation: RR Company receives $1,500 cash from B1 Company (phone number: 123456789) with the General ID 5

Customer or Supplier's Name	Address	E-mail	Postal Code

City	State	Country	

Person Handling: Manager:

Date: Date:

Figure 1-10   Original Proof of Sixth Transaction

Maybe you ask why I do not use the customer's phone number as a judging standard. Because RR Company may sale the inventory to this customer for several times and the General ID of a transaction is sole, I must choose the General ID as a judging standard.

From the Figure 1-10, the Reference box in the row with the account name of the "Account Receivable" is written into the relevant General ID of the "5" which is bold. The transaction sub-equation and the transaction mathematical sub-equation respectively are:

Cash (1) + Account receivable (1) = 0

$X101 + X104 = 0$

Because the account of the X101 has the two-level subaccount and the account of the X104 has the one-level subaccount (seeing the Figure 1-10), the one-level and the two-level expanding mathematical sub-equations are the following:

One-level sub-equation $X10102 + X10401 = 0$
Two-level sub-equation $X1010203 + X10401 = 0$

From the Figure 1-10, the X10102 is the "Operating activities" and X1010203 is the "Cash receipts from customers"; the X10401 is the "123456789".

The same method can be used to calculate the amounts of the parent accounts and their subaccounts.

For recording the transaction, I should just update the related parent accounts and their subaccounts information.

The Table 30 shows the general equation, the Table 31 shows the class accounts of the assets accounts (X1), the Table 32 shows the parent accounts of the "Cash" and the "Account receivable", the Table 33 shows the one-level subaccounts of the "Operating activities" and the "123456789", and the Table 34 shows the two-level subaccount "Cash receipts from customers", seeing the following tables.

Table 30 General equation

GeID	Transaction Date	General Equation	Left Amount	Right Amount	Explanation	Enter Date
1	2014-1-2	Cash(1): 10000 = Share capital(3): 4000 + Capital(3): 3000 + Capital(3): 3000	10000	10000	Ping Wang, Hua Li and Mike Newsome decide to open a RR trade business	2015-2-8
2	2014-1-3	Cash(1): -193 + Supplies(1): 193 = 0	0	0	Purchase of supplies	2015-2-8
3	2014-1-3	Cash(1): -47 = Expenses (5): -47	-47	-47	Cash payments for Hua Li's taxi fee expense	2015-2-8
4	2014-1-5	Cash(1): -670 +Inventory(1): 3670 = Account payable(2): 3000	3000	3000	RR purchases $3,670 inventory by $670 cash and other on credit from A1 company (phone number: 987654321)	2015-2-8
5	2014-1-5	Cash(1): 300 + Inventory(1): -1900 + Account receivable: 2230 = Revenues(4): 2530 + Expenses(5): -1900	630	630	RR sells $1,900 inventory to B1 Company (phone number: 123456789) for sales of $2,530 and receives $300 cash	2015-2-8
6	2014-1-28	Cash(1): 1500 + Account receivable(1): -1500 = 0	0	0	RR Company receives $1,500 cash from B1 Company (phone number: 123456789) with the General ID 5	2015-2-28
Total Amount			**13583**	**13583**		

Table 31 Class accounts

Assets (X1)

ID	Account Name (Mathematical Name)	Subtotal	Ref (Row)	Balance
1	Cash (X101)	Current assets,103	104	10890
2	Supplies (X102)	Current assets,103	106	193
3	Inventory (X103)	Current assets,103	108	1770
4	Account receivable (X104)	Current assets,103	110	730

Table 32 Parent accounts

Cash (X101)

ID	MultiName	Amount	Ref	Balance	GeID	SubFirst	SubSecond	SubThird	Unit
1	Cash receipts from owners<Financing activities	10000		10000	1	Financing activities	Cash receipts from owners		1
2	Cash payments for operating expenses<Operating activities	-193		9807	2	Operating activities	Cash payments for operating expenses		1
3	Cash payments for operating expenses<Operating activities	-47		9760	3	Operating activities	Cash payments for operating expenses		1
4	Cash payments to suppliers< Operating activities	-670		9090	4	Operating activities	Cash payments to suppliers		1
5	Cash receipts from customers< Operating activities	300		9390	5	Operating activities	Cash receipts from customers		1
6	Cash receipts from customers< Operating activities	1500	5	10890	6	Operating activities	Cash receipts from customers		1

Account receivable (X104)

ID	MultiName	Amount	Ref	Balance	GeID	SubFirst	SubSecond	SubThird	Unit
1	123456789	2230		2230	5	123456789			1
2	123456789	-1500	5	730	6	123456789			1

Table 33 One-level subaccounts

Operating activities (X10102) < Parent account: Cash (X101)

ID	MultiName	Amount	Ref	GeID	Transaction Date	Balance
1	Cash payments for operating expenses<Operating activities	-193		2	2014-1-3	-193
2	Cash payments for operating expenses<Operating activities	-47		3	2014-1-3	-240
3	Cash payments to suppliers< Operating activities	-670		4	2014-1-5	-910
4	Cash receipts from customers< Operating activities	300		5	2014-1-5	-610
5	Cash receipts from customers< Operating activities	1500	5	6	2014-1-28	890

123456789 (X10401) < Parent account: Account receivable (X104)

ID	MultiName	Amount	Ref	GeID	Transaction Date	Balance
1	123456789	2230		5	2014-1-5	2230
2	123456789	-1500	5	6	2014-1-28	730

Table 34 Two-level subaccount

Cash receipts from customers (X1010203) << Parent account: Cash (X101)

ID	MultiName	Amount	Ref	GeID	Transaction Date	Balance
1	Cash receipts from customers< Operating activities	300		5	2014-1-5	300
2	Cash receipts from customers< Operating activities	1500	5	6	2014-1-28	1800

I write the lowest subaccounts' amounts into their tables respectively and calculate their balances. The table of the "Cash receipts from customers (X1010203)" in the Table 34 is the lowest subaccount (two-level subaccount) of the parent account of the "Cash (X101)", so I write $1500 into the table of the "Cash receipts from customers (X1010203)" in the Table 34. The table of the "123456789 (X10401)" is the lowest subaccount (one-level subaccount) of the parent account of the "Account receivable (X104)" in the Table 33, so I write -$1500 and the related GeID "**5**" into the table of the "123456789 (X10401)" in the Table 33.

The table of the "Operating activities (X10102)" in the Table 33 can be gotten from the table of the "Cash receipts from customers (X1010203)" in the Table 34.

The two tables of the parent accounts of the "Cash (X101)" and the "Account receivable

(X104)" in the Table 32 can be gotten from the two tables of the "Operating activities (X10102)" and the "123456789 (X10401)" in the Table 33 respectively.

The balances of the table of the "Assets (X1)" in the Table 31 can be gotten from the two tables of the "Cash (X101)" and the "Account receivable (X104)" in the Table 32 respectively.

In addition, for getting the financial statements and checking information easily, I also create the Table 35 (by the order of the row number), the Table 36, and the Table 37 after recording the sixth transaction, seeing the following tables.

Table 35 Reference

ID	Account Name (Subtotal Name)	Row	GeID	Balance
1	**Current assets**	**103**	**1**	**13583**
2	Cash	104	1	10890
3	Supplies	106	2	193
4	Inventory	108	4	1770
5	Account receivable	110	5	730
6	**Current liabilities**	**203**	**4**	**3000**
7	Account payable	204	4	3000
8	**Owners' capital**	**303**	**1**	**10000**
9	Share capital	304	1	10000
10	**Revenues**	**403**	**5**	**2530**
11	Sales	404	5	2530
12	**Cost**	**431**	**5**	**-1900**
13	Cost of sales	432	5	-1900
14	**Operating and administrative expenses**	**453**	**3**	**-47**
15	Travelling expenses	454	3	-47

Table 36 Subtotal Name

ID	Subtotal Name	Row	GeID	Class
1	Current assets,103	103	1	1
2	Owners' capital,303	303	1	3
3	Operating and administrative expenses,453	453	3	5
4	Current liabilities,203	203	4	2
5	Revenues,403	403	5	4
5	Cost,431	431	5	5

Table 37 Multi-subaccounts

ID	Multi-subaccount Name	Parent Account	GeID	Class
1	Cash receipts from owners< Financing activities	Cash	1	1
2	Capital-Ping Wang	Share capital	1	3
3	Capital-Hua Li	Share capital	1	3
4	Capital-Mike Newsome	Share capital	1	3
5	Cash payments for operating expenses< Operating activities	Cash	2	1
6	N	Supplies	2	1
7	Hua Li-travelling< Purchase Department-travelling	Travelling expenses	3	5
8	Cash payments to suppliers< Operating activities	Cash	4	1
9	Inven111<Inven11<Inven1	Inventory	4	1
10	Inven112<Inven11<Inven1	Inventory	4	1
11	Inven121<Inven12<Inven1	Inventory	4	1
12	Inven122<Inven12<Inven1	Inventory	4	1
13	Inven13<Inven1	Inventory	4	1
14	987654321	Account payable	4	2
15	Cash receipts from customers< Operating activities	Cash	5	1
16	123456789	Account receivable	5	1
17	Xiao Zhou-sales	Sales	5	4
18	N	Cost of sales	5	5

So far, I have recorded 6 transactions' data. For checking whether the recording data is reliable and correct, I will do the following three calculations.

- Check whether the dynamic accounting equation is equal.

    From the Table 30, when the 6 general equations are added together, I get the left amount $13583 and the right amount $13583 of the dynamic accounting equation on February 28, 2014. These two amounts are equal.

- Check whether the sum of all assets accounts' balances is equal to the sum of all liabilities accounts, all equity accounts, all incomes accounts, and all expenses accounts' balances.

    1. For all assets accounts

        From the Table 32, I get that the balance of the parent account "Cash" is $10,890 and the balance of the parent account "Account receivable" is $730.

        From the table 25, I get that the balance of the parent account "Inventory" is

$1,770.

From the Table 8, I get that the balance of the parent account "Supplies" is $193.

Therefore, the sum of the assets accounts' balances is $13,583 (= $10,890 + $730 + $1,770 + $193).

Of course, I can also get that the sum of the assets accounts' balances is $13,583 from the table "Assets (X1)" in the Table 31.

2. For all liabilities accounts

From the Table 18, I get that the balance of the parent account "Account payable" is $3,000.

Therefore, the total amount of the liabilities account's balance is $3,000.

Of course, I can also get that the sum of the liabilities account's balance is $3,000 from the table "Liabilities (X2)" in the Table 17.

3. For all shareholders' equity accounts

From the Table 3, I get that the balance of the parent account "Share capital" is $10,000.

Therefore, the sum of the shareholders' equity account's balance is $10,000.

Of course, I can also get that the sum of the shareholders' equity account's balance is $10,000 from the table "Shareholders' equity (X3)" in the Table 2.

4. For all revenues accounts

From the Table 25, I get that the balance of the parent account "Sales" is $2,530.

Therefore, the sum of the revenues account's balance is $2,530.

Of course, I can also get that the sum of the revenues account's balance is $2,530 from the table "Revenues (X4)" in the Table 24.

5. For all expenses accounts

From the Table 25, I get that the balance of the parent account "Cost of sales" is -$1,900.

From the Table 13, I get that the balance of the parent account "Travelling expenses" is -$47.

So, the sum of the expenses accounts' balances is -$1,947 (= -$1,900 -$47).

Of course, I can also get that the sum of the expenses accounts' balances is -$1,947 from the table "Expenses (X5)" in the Table 24.

The sum of all assets accounts is $13,583. The sum of all liabilities accounts, all shareholders' equity accounts, all revenues accounts, and all expenses accounts is $13,583 (= $3,000 + $10,000 + $2,530 - $1,947).

These two sum amounts are equal. They are $13,583.

- After the previous two steps are correct, I check whether the left (or right) amount of the dynamic accounting equation is equal to the sum of all assets accounts' balances (or the sum of all liabilities, all equity accounts, all incomes accounts, and all expenses accounts' balances).

Obviously, the requirement is satisfied.

The above three requirements are satisfied, so the mathematical accounting model is reliable and correct.

Maybe, you asked that the mathematical accounting model is so complicated. Yes. If a business company has many subaccounts, it is very difficult to record these transactions.

However, we are lucky. With development of computer and database technology, most work in the mathematical accounting model can be done by the computer. Therefore, it is very easy to record these transactions by using of the MathAccounting software which is based on this mathematical accounting model. The only parent accounts' tables are created in the database and all subaccounts' tables will be gotten by using of the database query in the MathAccounting software, so what you must know is just to fill in the original proof of a transaction. It is easy?

Chapter 2

Introduction of MathAccounting Software

Based on above mathematical accounting model, I have developed and completed the MathAccounting Software by using the Visual Basic 2012 language and the SQL Server 2012 database in February 2015.

The MathAccounting software has little limitation, just like the equation of the "1 + 1 = 2" which may be that one person plus one person equals two persons or one apple plus one apple equals two apples, so the MathAccounting software can be used by all economic entities regardless of their size, nature of business, or form of business organization without any altering.

The MathAccounting software has the four function models: Transactions, Reports, Backup/Restore, and Maintenances. I suggest that the names of all accounts and subaccounts are only consisted of English alphabets, number, colon, and blank space when you enter these names. I will introduce the four function model below.

In this version of MathAccounting software, there are some limitations (from theory, the numbers are infinite):

- The maximum number of entries in each transaction is eight, which means that there are maximum eight terms (items) in a sub-equation (general equation).
- The maximum number of customers or suppliers is twenty.
- The maximum level number in a multi-subaccount name of every parent account is three. Its form in the "MultiSubaccount Name" box is defined as the "three-level subaccount<two-level subaccount<one-level subaccount".

After executing the software, I can get the Figure 2-1, seeing the next page.

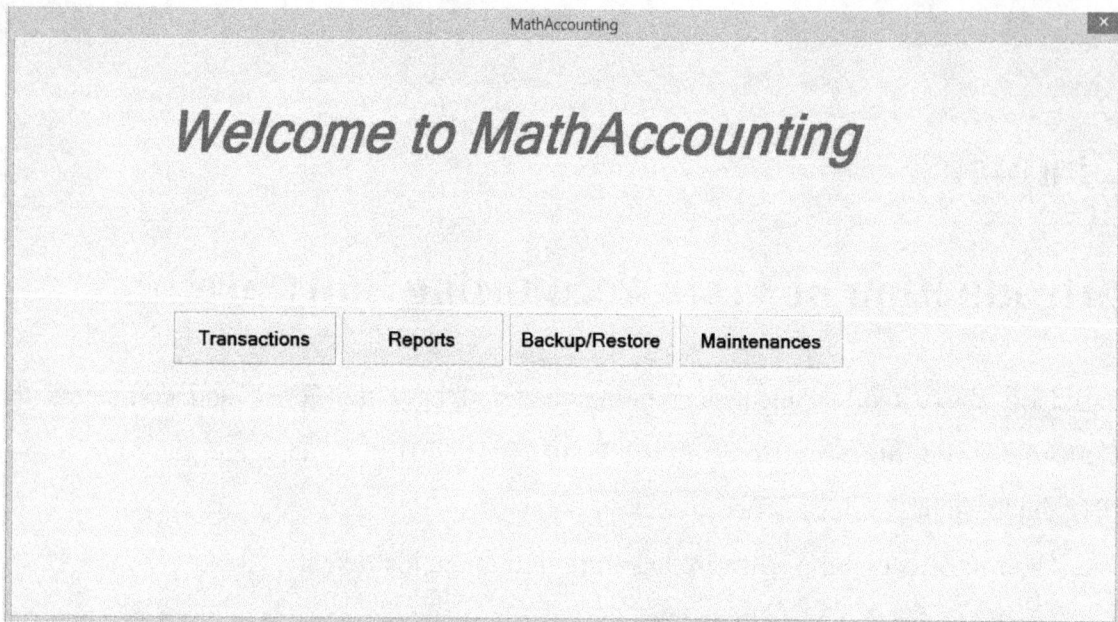

Figure 2-1   MathAccounting Interface

There are the four boxes of the functions in the Figure 2-1. The Transactions box is to enter each transaction and to design your income statements, balance sheet, cash flows and so on. The Reports box is to get all information about all parent accounts, subaccounts, and company performance. The Backup/Restore box is to backup and restore database. The Maintenances box is to delete the useless parent accounts or alter some mistakes (only names). However, I must emphasize such a fact that entering or altering of every amount can be only completed by using of entering a transaction in the Transaction function model.

2.1 Transactions function model

After clicking the Transactions box, I can get the Figure 2-2 on the next page.

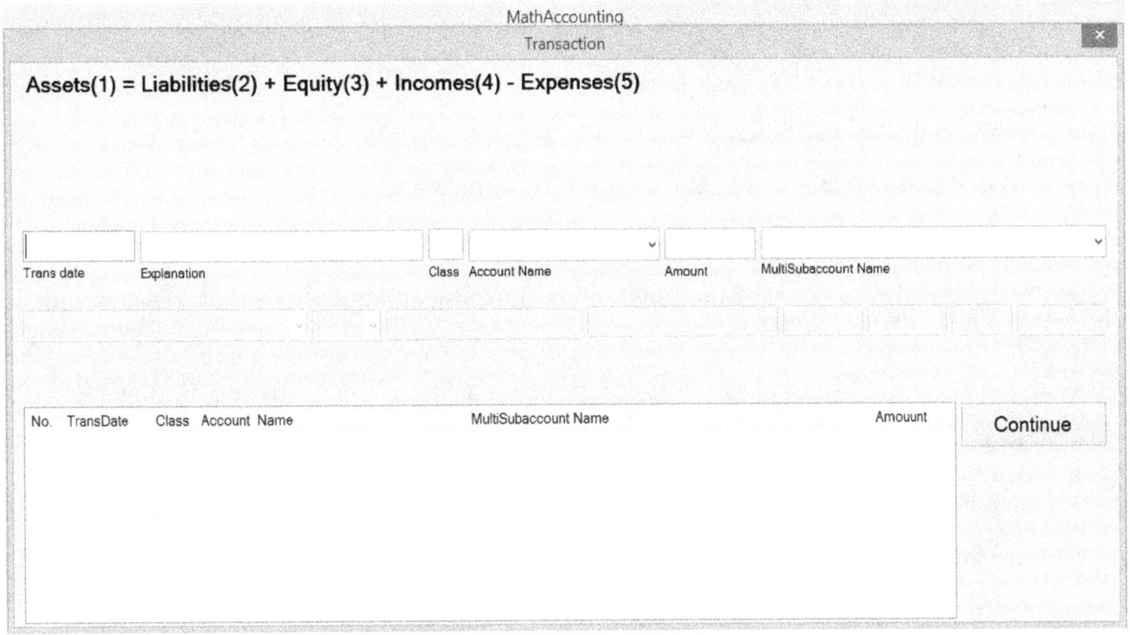

Figure 2-2   Transaction Entering Interface

There are three rows of boxes in the Figure 2-2, but you can only see the two rows of the boxes now. The other row of box or boxes can be shown in satisfying special requirement, such as a new account being entered.

There are six boxes in the first row.

- Trans Date of box: enter transaction date.

- Explanation of box: enter transaction's explanation including any invoice number.

- Class of box: enter only one number of the one to five.

- Account Name of box: enter parent account name which will appear in the income statement and the balance sheet.

- Amount of box: enter an amount. Increasing balance is the " + " (you can omit it); decreasing balance is the " – ".

- MultiSubaccount Name of box: enter a multi-subaccount name. Its form is the "three-level subaccount<two-level subaccount<one-level subaccount".

There are two boxes in third row.

- Big box: it only shows you how many entries you have entered in a transaction. If the sub-equation is equal, a general equation will appear under the dynamic accounting equation, which means that a transaction has entered into database completely and correctly. Meanwhile, the contents in the boxes of the first and second rows will disappear to be ready for a new transaction.

- Small box: click it to continue current transaction or begin a new transaction.

The second row boxes' functions will be introduced later while they are enabled.

Now, let me enter the following five transactions by using of the MathAccounting software.

- Investment by owners. On January 2, 2014, Ping Wang, Hua Li and Mike Newsome decide to open a RR trade business, so Ping Wang invests $4,000 cash in business, and Hua Li and Mike Newsome each invest $3,000 cash in business.

Seeing the Figure 1-5 again which shows the original proof of this transaction. The sub-equation can be written as following:

Cash (1): 10000 = Share capital (3): 4000 + Share capital (3): 3000
+ Share capital (3): 3000

After I enter the "Cash" into the Account Name box, the Subtotal and Reference boxes are enabled. The main functions of these two boxes are to build the balance sheet and income statements. In this transaction, I enter the "Current assets, 103" into the Subtotal Name box and the "104" into the Reference box, which shows in the Figure 2-3 on the next page.

The Multisubaccount Name box can be used to build a cash flows statement by entering the cash account's one-level subaccount and two-level subaccount into the Multisubaccount Name box. From the Figure 2-3 or the Figure 1-5, its entering form is the "Cash receipts from owners< Financing activities".

Similarly, I can build the account flows statement for every account if it has the two-level accounts. The detail of the account flows statement will be introduced later.

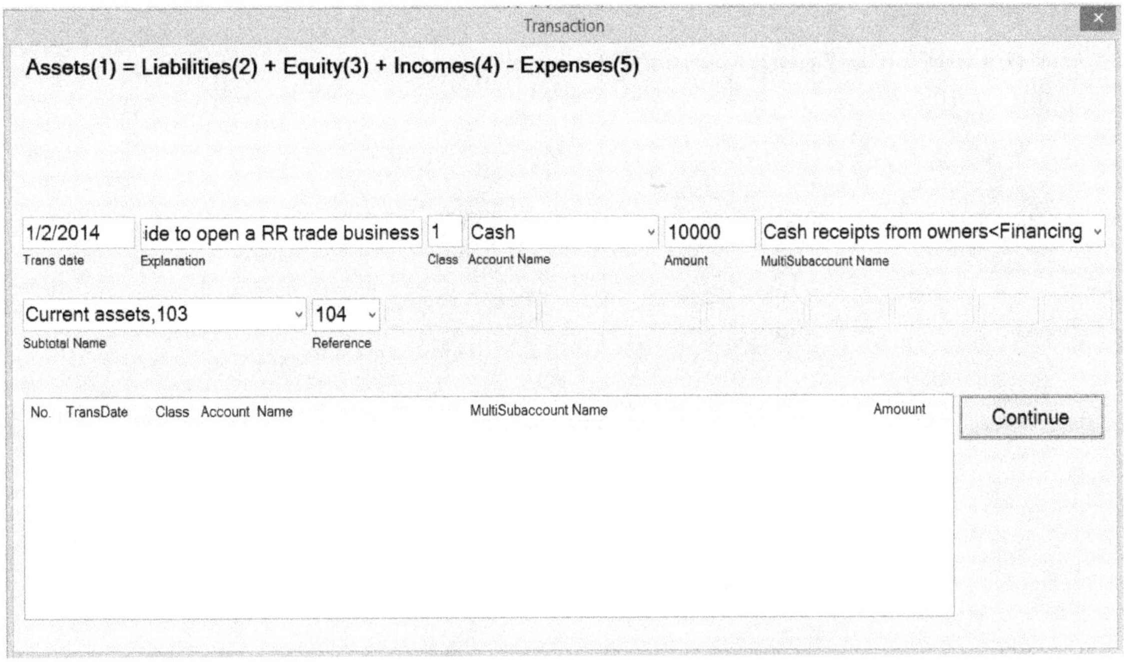

Transaction

Assets(1) = Liabilities(2) + Equity(3) + Incomes(4) - Expenses(5)

1/2/2014	ide to open a RR trade business	1	Cash	⌄	10000	Cash receipts from owners<Financing ⌄
Trans date	Explanation	Class	Account Name		Amount	MultiSubaccount Name

Current assets,103	⌄	104	⌄
Subtotal Name		Reference	

No.	TransDate	Class	Account	Name	MultiSubaccount Name	Amouunt

Continue

Figure   2-3   Entering Cash Account

Clicking Continue box, I get the Figure 2-4, seeing the next page. The Figure 2-4 is different from the Figure 2-3. One is that some boxes are empty and the cursor is focus on the Class box, which tells me that this entry is completed and new entry can begin. Another is that what I just entered appears in the big box.

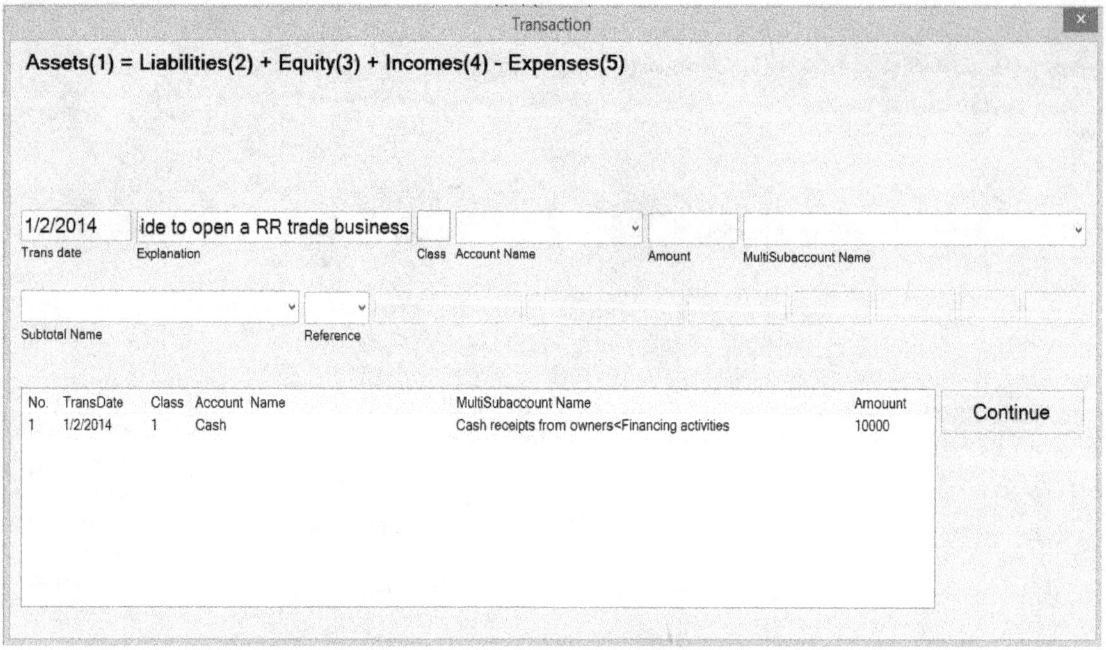

Figure 2-4 Entered Cash Interface

Because the "Share capital" account has three one-level subaccounts, I must enter these one-level subaccounts separately. The Figure 2-5, the Figure 2-6, and the Figure 2-7 show the three entries respectively, seeing the following pages.

From the Figure 2-5, the Subtotal Name box and the Reference box keep enabled after entering "Share capital" into the Account Name box because the "Share capital" is a new account. I enter the "Owners' capital, 303" and the "304" into the Subtotal Name box and the Reference box" respectively.

From the Figure 2-6, the Subtotal Name box and Reference box are not enabled after entering "Share capital" into the Account Name box because the "Share capital" account has existed in the database.

From the Figure 2-7, the Subtotal Name box and Reference box are also not enabled after entering "Share capital" into the Account Name box because of the same reason. A general equation appears under the dynamic accounting equation after clicking the Continue box and the cursor is focus on the Trans date box, which actually means that a transaction has completed correctly and the entered information has saved into database.

Transaction

Assets(1) = Liabilities(2) + Equity(3) + Incomes(4) - Expenses(5)

1/2/2014	ide to open a RR trade business	3	Share capital	⌄	4000	Capital-Ping Wang	⌄
Trans date	Explanation	Class	Account Name		Amount	MultiSubaccount Name	

Owners' capital,303	⌄	304	⌄
Subtotal Name		Reference	

No.	TransDate	Class	Account Name	MultiSubaccount Name	Amouunt	
1	1/2/2014	1	Cash	Cash receipts from owners<Financing activities	10000	Continue

Transaction

Assets(1) = Liabilities(2) + Equity(3) + Incomes(4) - Expenses(5)

1/2/2014	ide to open a RR trade business			⌄			⌄
Trans date	Explanation	Class	Account Name		Amount	MultiSubaccount Name	

	⌄		⌄
Subtotal Name		Reference	

No.	TransDate	Class	Account Name	MultiSubaccount Name	Amouunt	
1	1/2/2014	1	Cash	Cash receipts from owners<Financing activities	10000	Continue
		3	Share capital	Capital-Ping Wang	4000	

Figure 2-5   Entering First One-level Subaccount

Transaction ✕

Assets(1) = Liabilities(2) + Equity(3) + Incomes(4) - Expenses(5)

1/2/2014	ide to open a RR trade business	3	Share capital ⌄	3000	Capital-Hua Li ⌄
Trans date	Explanation	Class	Account Name	Amount	MultiSubaccount Name

No.	TransDate	Class	Account Name	MultiSubaccount Name	Amouunt	
1	1/2/2014	1	Cash	Cash receipts from owners<Financing activities	10000	Continue
		3	Share capital	Capital-Ping Wang	4000	

Transaction ✕

Assets(1) = Liabilities(2) + Equity(3) + Incomes(4) - Expenses(5)

1/2/2014	ide to open a RR trade business		⌄		⌄
Trans date	Explanation	Class	Account Name	Amount	MultiSubaccount Name

	⌄		⌄		
Subtotal Name		Reference			

No.	TransDate	Class	Account Name	MultiSubaccount Name	Amouunt	
1	1/2/2014	1	Cash	Cash receipts from owners<Financing activities	10000	Continue
		3	Share capital	Capital-Ping Wang	4000	
		3	Share capital	Capital-Hua Li	3000	

Figure 2-6　Entering Second One-level Subaccount

Transaction

Assets(1) = Liabilities(2) + Equity(3) + Incomes(4) - Expenses(5)

1/2/2014	ide to open a RR trade business	3	Share capital	∨	3000	Capital-Mike Newsome	∨
Trans date	Explanation	Class	Account Name		Amount	MultiSubaccount Name	

No.	TransDate	Class	Account Name	MultiSubaccount Name	Amouunt	
1	1/2/2014	1	Cash	Cash receipts from owners<Financing activities	10000	**Continue**
		3	Share capital	Capital-Ping Wang	4000	
		3	Share capital	Capital-Hua Li	3000	

Transaction

Assets(1) = Liabilities(2) + Equity(3) + Incomes(4) - Expenses(5)

Cash(1): 10000 = Share capital(3): 4000 + Share capital(3): 3000 + Share capital(3): 3000

				∨			∨
Trans date	Explanation	Class	Account Name		Amount	MultiSubaccount Name	

Subtotal Name		Reference	

No.	TransDate	Class	Account Name	MultiSubaccount Name	Amouunt	
1	1/2/2014	1	Cash	Cash receipts from owners<Financing activities	10000	**Continue**
		3	Share capital	Capital-Ping Wang	4000	
		3	Share capital	Capital-Hua Li	3000	
		3	Share capital	Capital-Mike Newsome	3000	

Figure 2-7   Entering Third One-level Subaccount and Completed a Transaction

- Purchase of supplies by cash. On January 3, 2014, RR purchases some supplies by $193 cash from the AA Company.

Seeing the Figure 1-6 again which shows the original proof of this transaction.

The transaction sub-equation is:

Cash (1): -193 + Supplies (1): 193 = 0

After entering the "Cash" account's information, I get the following Figure 2-8.

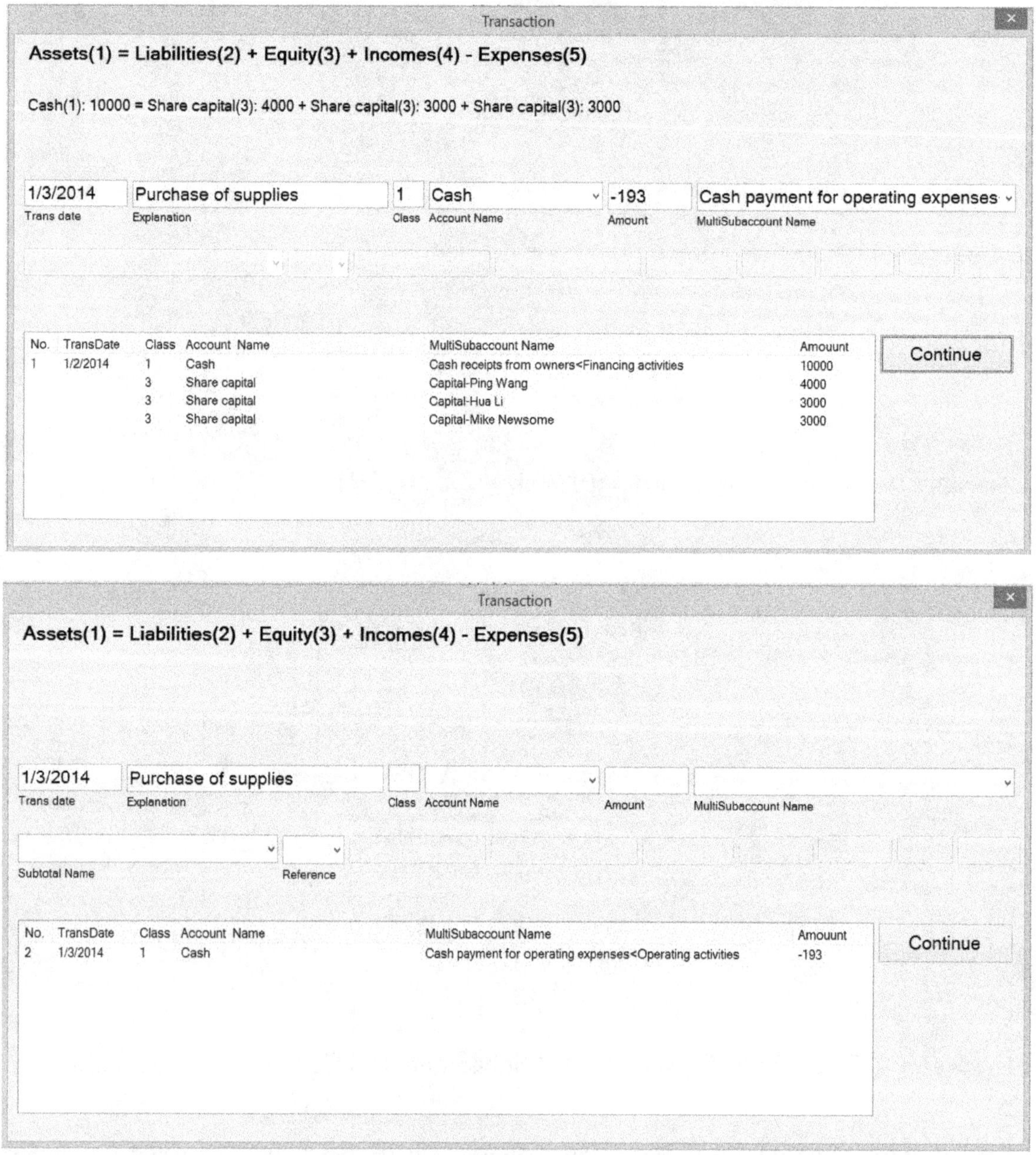

Figure 2-8   Entering Cash Account

Again, the Multisubaccount Name box can be used to build a cash flows statement by entering the cash account's one-level subaccount and two-level subaccount into the Multisubaccount Name box. From the Figure 2-8 or the Figure 1-6, its entering form is the "Cash payments for operating expenses< Operating activities".

Entering the "Supplies" account into the Account Name box, I get the Figure 2-9, seeing the next page.

From the Figure 2-9, the "Supplies" account is a new account, so I enter row number 106 into the Reference box. Of course, you may enter number105 or108 if you like. There is a letter of the "n" in the Multisubaccount Name box, which means that the "Supplies" account has not any subaccount.

A general equation appears under the dynamic accounting equation in the Figure 2-9 on the next page, which means that the transaction has entered into the database correctly.

- Cash payments for Hua Li's taxi fee expense. On same day, Hua Li takes taxi to carry on the supplies for $47 cash.

The sub-equation is:

Cash (1): -47 = - Travelling expenses (5): 47

Seeing the Figure 1-7 again which shows the original proof of this transaction.

The "Travelling expenses" account is a new account, so the Subtotal Name box must be entered. The "Travelling expenses" account must be under the row of the "Gross Margin" whose number is 451, so the row number of the "Travelling expenses" account should be greater than number 451. If the Subtotal name is the "Operating and Administrative expenses, 453", the number in the Reference box should obviously be 454 (or 456 if you like), seeing the Figure 2-10 which follows the Figure 2-9.

Transaction

Assets(1) = Liabilities(2) + Equity(3) + Incomes(4) - Expenses(5)

1/3/2014	Purchase of supplies	1	Supplies	˅	193	n	˅
Trans date	Explanation	Class	Account Name		Amount	MultiSubaccount Name	

Current assets,103	˅	106	˅
Subtotal Name		Reference	

No.	TransDate	Class	Account Name	MultiSubaccount Name	Amouunt	
2	1/3/2014	1	Cash	Cash payment for operating expenses<Operating activities	-193	Continue

Transaction

Assets(1) = Liabilities(2) + Equity(3) + Incomes(4) - Expenses(5)

Cash(1): -193 + Supplies(1): 193 = 0

				˅			˅
Trans date	Explanation	Class	Account Name		Amount	MultiSubaccount Name	

	˅		˅
Subtotal Name		Reference	

No.	TransDate	Class	Account Name	MultiSubaccount Name	Amouunt	
2	1/3/2014	1	Cash	Cash payment for operating expenses<Operating activities	-193	Continue
		1	Supplies	n	193	

Figure 2-9   Entering Supplies Account

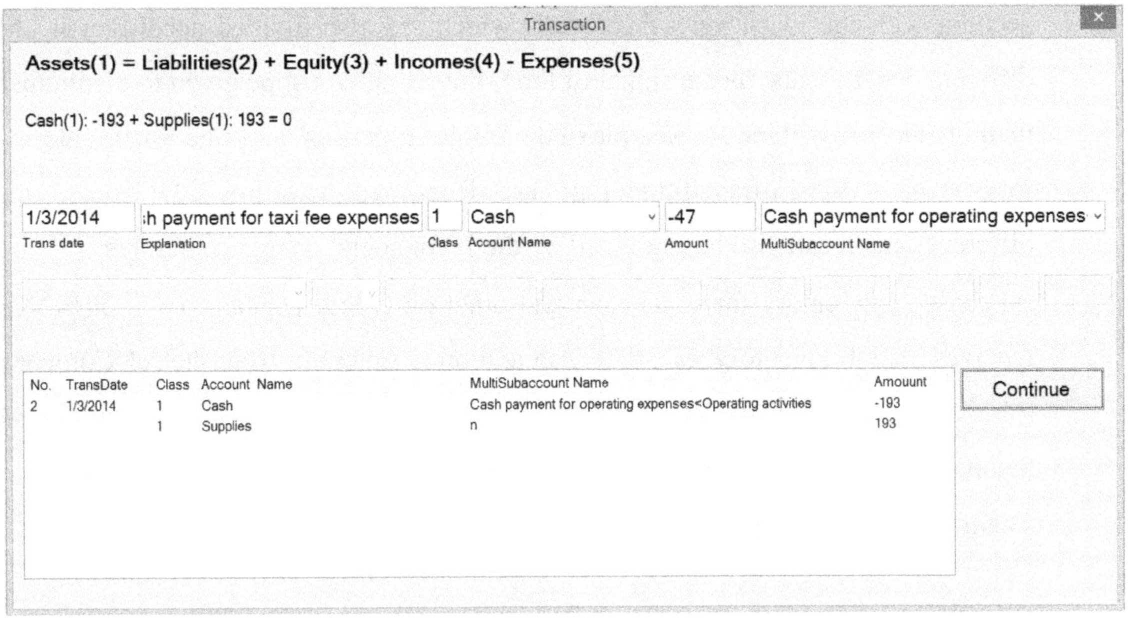

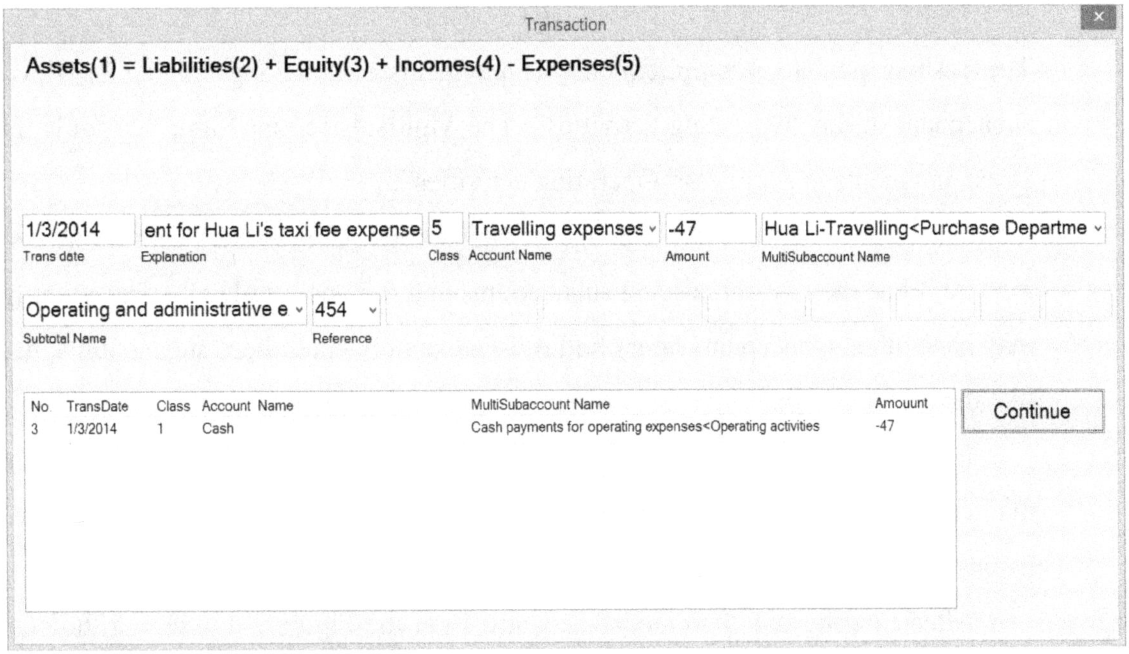

Figure 2-10   Entering Cash and Travelling expenses accounts

The "Travelling expenses" account has the two-level subaccounts, such as the "Different person< Purchase department", the "Different person< Office department", and the "Different person< Sales department", so its entering form should be the "Hua Li <Purchase department". However, if there are any other parent

account with the two-level subaccounts which are also divided according to the different departments, then a signal of the "-travelling" must be given to distinguish them. Later, you will see an example of the "Other expenses" account. So, its entering form is the "Hua Li-travelling< Purchase department-travelling". Of course, the different person can also be presented by the ID or social insurance number.

- Purchase of inventory for some cash and other on credit. On January 5, 2014, RR receives $3,670 inventory for $670 cash and other on credit from the A1 Company (phone number: 987654321).

Seeing the Figure 1-8 again which shows the original proof of this transaction.

The transaction sub-equation is:

Cash (1): -670 + Inventory (1): 3670 = Account payable (2): 3000

The cash is paid to a supplier, but the payments still belongs to the one-level subaccount of the "Operating activities". The Multisubaccount Name's form is the "Cash payments to suppliers< Operating activities".

The "Inventory" account belongs to the subtotal name of the "Current assets" too and it has the four three-level subaccounts and the one two-level subaccount (it may have other subaccounts later), so I must separately enter these subaccounts, just like the previous "Share capital" account.

For understanding the relationship of these subaccounts easily, I use mathematical language to describe them. In real environment, you can use actual names to replace these logical names.

After entering the "Inventory" account, I get the Figure 2-11, seeing the next page.

Transaction

Assets(1) = Liabilities(2) + Equity(3) + Incomes(4) - Expenses(5)

1/5/2014	ɔany(phone number:987654321)	1	Inventory ⌄	10*165	Inven111<inven11<inven1 ⌄
Trans date	Explanation	Class	Account Name	Amount	MultiSubaccount Name

Current assets,103 ⌄	108 ⌄
Subtotal Name	Reference

No.	TransDate	Class	Account Name	MultiSubaccount Name	Amouunt	
4	1/5/2014	1	Cash	Cash payment to suppliers<Operating activities	-670	Continue

Transaction

Assets(1) = Liabilities(2) + Equity(3) + Incomes(4) - Expenses(5)

1/5/2014	ɔany(phone number:987654321)		⌄		⌄
Trans date	Explanation	Class	Account Name	Amount	MultiSubaccount Name

⌄	⌄
Subtotal Name	Reference

No.	TransDate	Class	Account Name	MultiSubaccount Name	Amouunt	
4	1/5/2014	1	Cash	Cash payment to suppliers<Operating activities	-670	Continue
		1	Inventory	Inven111<inven11<inven1	1650	
		1	Inventory	Inven112<inven11<inven1	900	
		1	Inventory	inven121<Inven12<Inven1	520.0	
		1	Inventory	Inven122<Inven12<Inven1	330	
		1	Inventory	Inven13<Inven1	270	

Figure 2-11   Entering Inventory Account

After entering the "Account payable" account, I get the Figure 2-12, seeing the next page. From the Figure 2-12, there is a big change which is that the other boxes of the second row are enabled now. These boxes are used to enter customers' or suppliers' information. Here is a supplier. The "Account payable" account is a new account, and its subtotal name should be the "Current liabilities". I give the row number of the subtotal name is 203, so the Reference box is 204. In addition, a general equation appears under the dynamic accounting equation, which means the transaction is completed correctly.

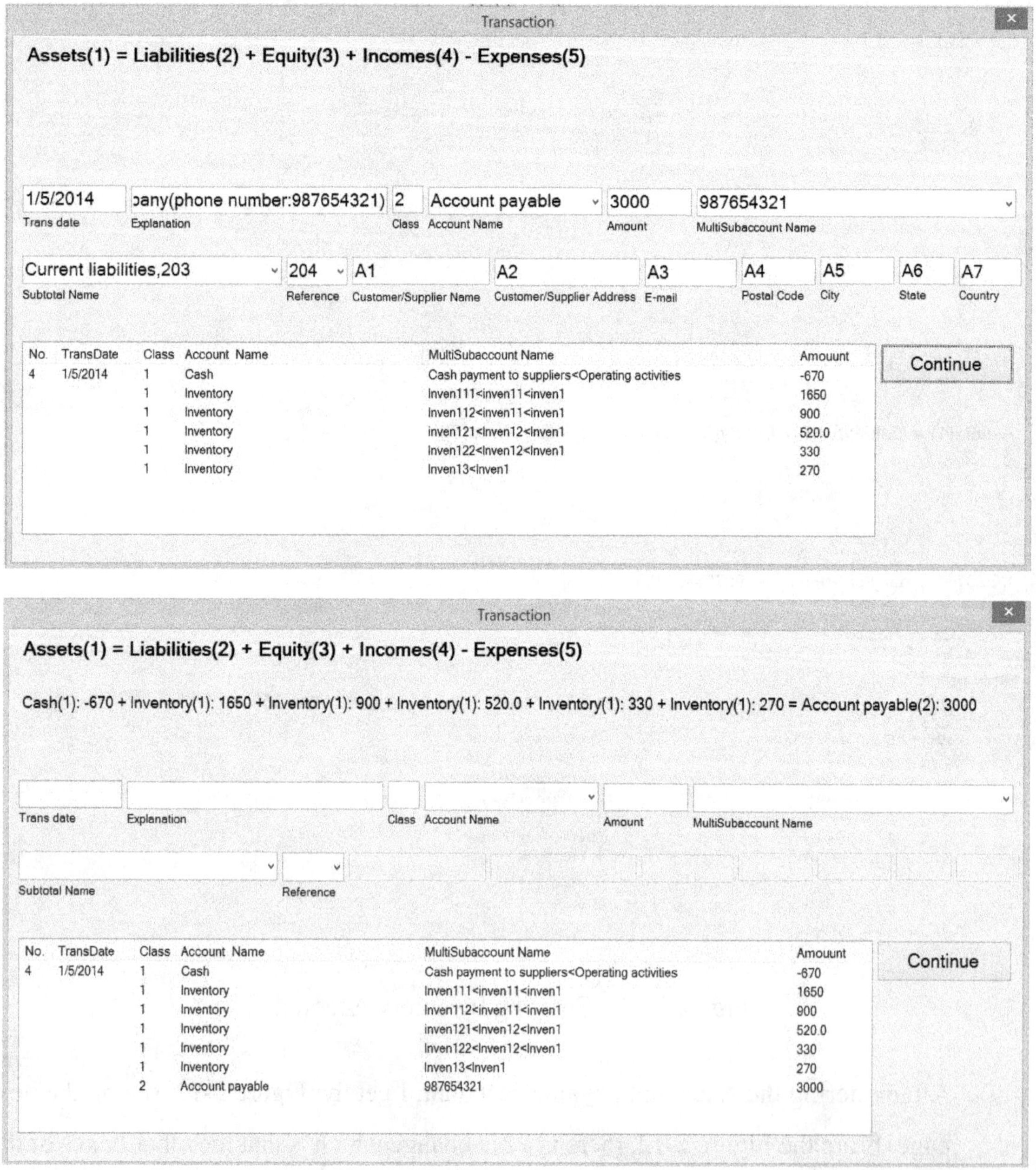

Figure 2-12   Entering Account Payable

- Xiao Zhou sales for some cash and other on credit. On January 5, 2014, RR sells $1,900 inventory for sales of $2,530 to B1 Company (phone number: 123456789), and receives cash 300.

Seeing the Figure 1-9 again which shows the original proof of this transaction. The transaction sub-equation is:

Cash (1): 300 +Inventory (1): -1900 + Account receivable (1): 2230 = Sales (4): 2530 - Cost of sales (5): 1900

The cash is received from a customer, so the Multisubaccount Name box is entered into the "Cash receipts from customers< Operating activities", which is different from the previous cash entry. Its two-level subaccount is the "Cash receipts from customers".

The entries of the inventory are similar as previous inventory's entries, but please pay attentions of the fact that their amounts all should be negative because they are sold and the amounts decrease.

The entry of the "Account receivable" is similar as previous "Account payable" entry. Its subtotal name is the "Current assets,103" and its row number is 110.

After entering the "Sales" account into the Account Name box and clicking the Continue Box, I get the Figure 2-13, seeing the next page.

From the Figure 2-13, an information box appears. It tells me that 7 entries have been entered and what the amounts of the left and the right of the sub-equation are, so I must enter correct amount in the last entry (eighth entry) to make the two sides of the sub-equation equal.

A transaction has only a maximum number of eight entries in this version of the MathAccountion software. From theory, a transaction can have infinite entries. I will increase the entries' number of a transaction in later version of the MathAccounting software.

Transaction

Assets(1) = Liabilities(2) + Equity(3) + Incomes(4) - Expenses(5)

1/5/2014	f $2530 and receives $300 cash	4	Sales	⌄	2530	Xiao Zhou-Sales	⌄
Trans date	Explanation	Class	Account Name		Amount	MultiSubaccount Name	

Revenues,403	⌄	404	⌄
Subtotal Name		Reference	

×

Last entry must make the equation equal. Left of euation = 630.0; Right of equation = 2530.

[OK]

No.	TransDate	Class	Account Name		Amouunt	
5	1/5/2014	1	Cash		300	Continue
		1	Inventory		-910	
		1	Inventory	Inven112<inven11<inven1	-520	
		1	Inventory	inven121<Inven12<Inven1	-300.0	
		1	Inventory	Inven122<Inven12<Inven1	-170	
		1	Account receivable	123456789	2230	
		4	Sales	Xiao Zhou-Sales	2530	

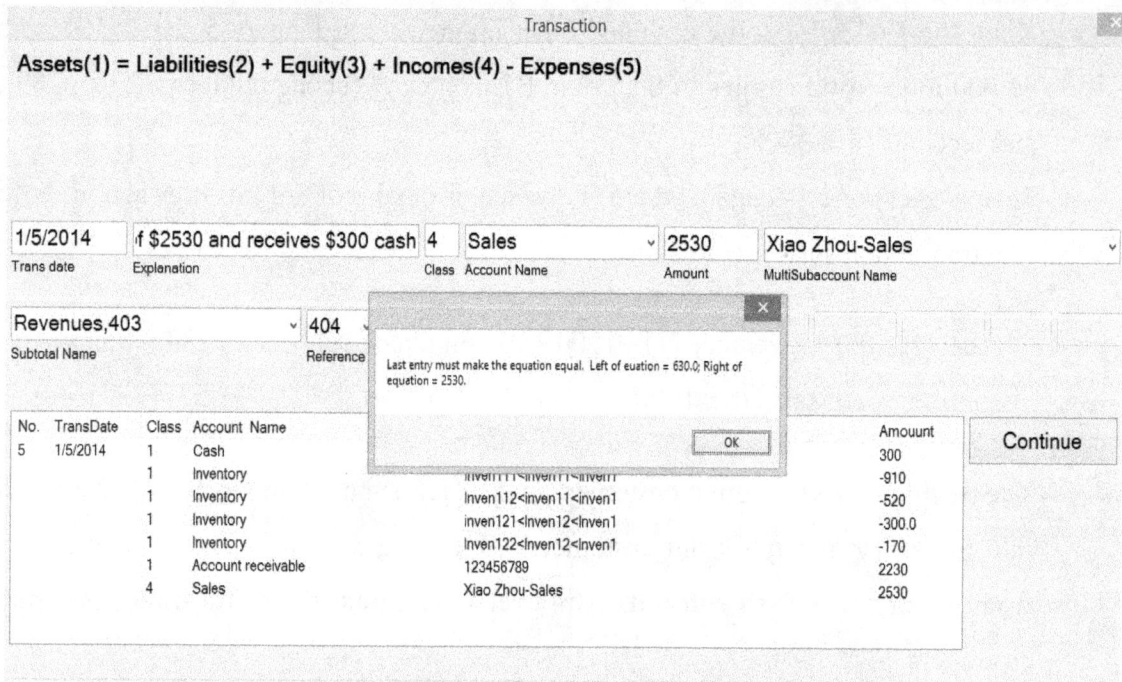

Figure 2-13   Information Box Appearing

Entering the "Cost of sales" account into the Account Name box, I gets the Figure 2-14 on the next page. From the Figure 2-14, the "Cost of sales" account is a new account and should appear under the Subtotal name of the "Revenues" (its row number is 403), so the row number of the Subtotal name should be 431 and the reference box's number be 432. In addition, a general equation appears under the dynamic accounting equation, which means that the transaction is completed correctly.

Before entering more transactions, let us take a rest and look at the other three function models: Reports, Backup/Restore, and Maintenances.

Transaction ×

Assets(1) = Liabilities(2) + Equity(3) + Incomes(4) - Expenses(5)

1/5/2014	456789), and receives cash 300	5	Cost of sales	-1900	n
Trans date	Explanation	Class	Account Name	Amount	MultiSubaccount Name

Cost,431	432
Subtotal Name	Reference

No	TransDate	Class	Account Name	MultiSubaccount Name	Amouunt	
1	1/5/2014	1	Cash	Cash receipts from customers<Operating activities	300	Continue
		1	Inventory	Inven111 < Inven11 < Inven1	-910	
		1	Inventory	Inven112 < Inven11 < Inven1	-520	
		1	Inventory	Inven121 < Inven12 < Inven1	-300.0	
		1	Inventory	Inven122 < Inven12 < Inven1	-170	
		1	Account receivable	123456789	2230	
		4	Sales	Xiao Zhou-sales	2530	

Transaction ×

Assets(1) = Liabilities(2) + Equity(3) + Incomes(4) - Expenses(5)

Cash(1): 300 + Inventory(1): -910 + Inventory(1): -520 + Inventory(1): -300.0 + Inventory(1): -170 + Account receivable(1): 2230 = Sales(4): 2530 - Cos

Trans date	Explanation	Class	Account Name	Amount	MultiSubaccount Name

Subtotal Name	Reference

No	TransDate	Class	Account Name	MultiSubaccount Name	Amouunt	
1	1/5/2014	1	Cash	Cash receipts from customers<Operating activities	300	Continue
		1	Inventory	Inven111 < Inven11 < Inven1	-910	
		1	Inventory	Inven112 < Inven11 < Inven1	-520	
		1	Inventory	Inven121 < Inven12 < Inven1	-300.0	
		1	Inventory	Inven122 < Inven12 < Inven1	-170	
		1	Account receivable	123456789	2230	
		4	Sales	Xiao Zhou-sales	2530	
		5	Cost of sales	n	-1900	

Figure 2-14   Entering Cost of Sales Account

2.2 Reports function model

The Reports function model does not check anything and only shows you all information you have entered into the database in the Transactions function model. After calculating or categorizing behind the screen, the information is shown by the tables.

Executing the MathAccounting software and clicking the Reports Box, I get the Figure 2-15. There are 18 small boxes on the right of the screen, which means that you can get 18 different information tables. When I click a box, I may be required to enter simple information, such as an account name. Entering the capital case letters or the lower case letters does not matter.

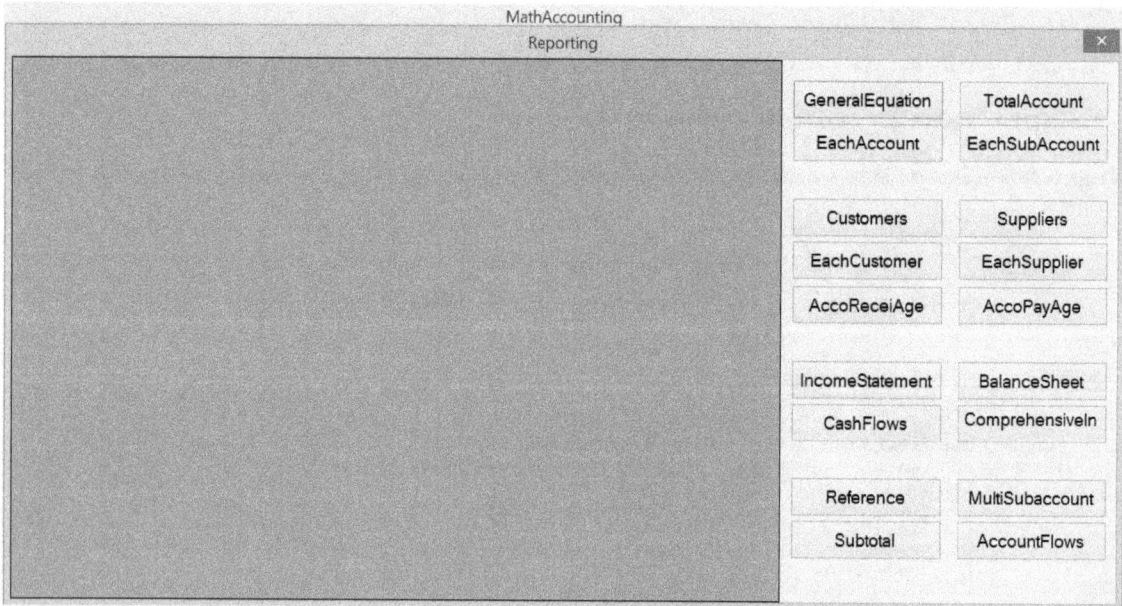

Figure 2-15   Reports Function Model Interface

Clicking the GeneralEquation box, I get the Figure 2-16, seeing the next page. The figure 2-16 shows me five general equations or sub-equations and other information I entered before. The General ID is a very useful parameter which is often quoted or referenced by other processes or the tables except for recording total number of the transactions I have entered. Scrolling rightly, I can get more information.

General ID	Transaction Date	General Equation	Left Amount	Right Amount
1	2014-01-02	Cash(1): 10000 = Share capital(3): 4000 + Share capital(3): 3000 + Sh...	$10,000.00	$10,000
2	2014-01-03	Cash(1): -193 + Supplies(1): 193 = 0	$0.00	$0
3	2014-01-03	Cash(1): -47 = - Travelling(5): 47	-$47.00	-$47
4	2014-01-05	Cash(1): -670 + Inventory(1): 1650 + Inventory(1): 900 + Inventory(1): 52...	$3,000.00	$3,000
5	2014-01-05	Cash(1): 300 + Inventory(1): -910 + Inventory(1): -520 + Inventory(1): -3...	$630.00	$630

Figure 2-16   General Equation Table

Clicking the TotalAccount box, I get the Figure 2-17, seeing the next page. The Figure 2-17 requires me to enter one number of the class number 1-5. If entering "1" and clicking the OK box, I get the Figure 2-18, following Figure 2-17. There are four accounts, their subtotal names, and their balances in the Figure 2-18. Similarly, I can get other classes' accounts.

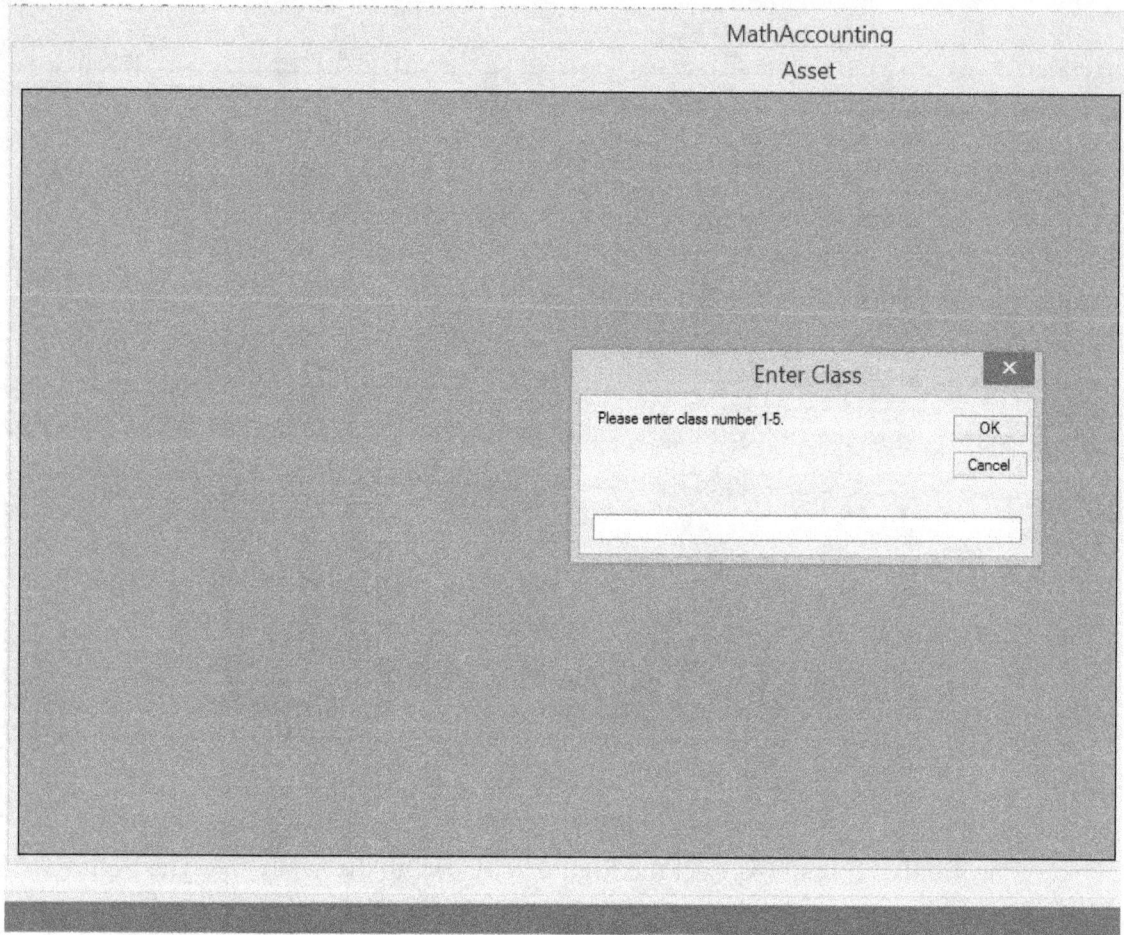

Figure 2-17   Entering Class Number

Asset

Name	Subtotal	Balance
Account receivable	Current assests,103	$2,230.00
Cash	Current assests,103	$9,390.00
Inventory	Current assests,103	$1,770.00
Supplies	Current assests,103	$193.00

Figure 2-18 Total Assets Accounts Table

Clicking the EachAccount box, I get the Figure 2-19 which requires me to enter an account name, seeing the next page. After entering the "iNvenTory" and clicking the OK box, I get the Figure 2-20, following the Figure 2-19. The ID number is total entries of the "Inventory", which is different from the General ID obviously.

MathAccounting

General Equation

Enter Account ×

Please enter account name.

OK

Cancel

|

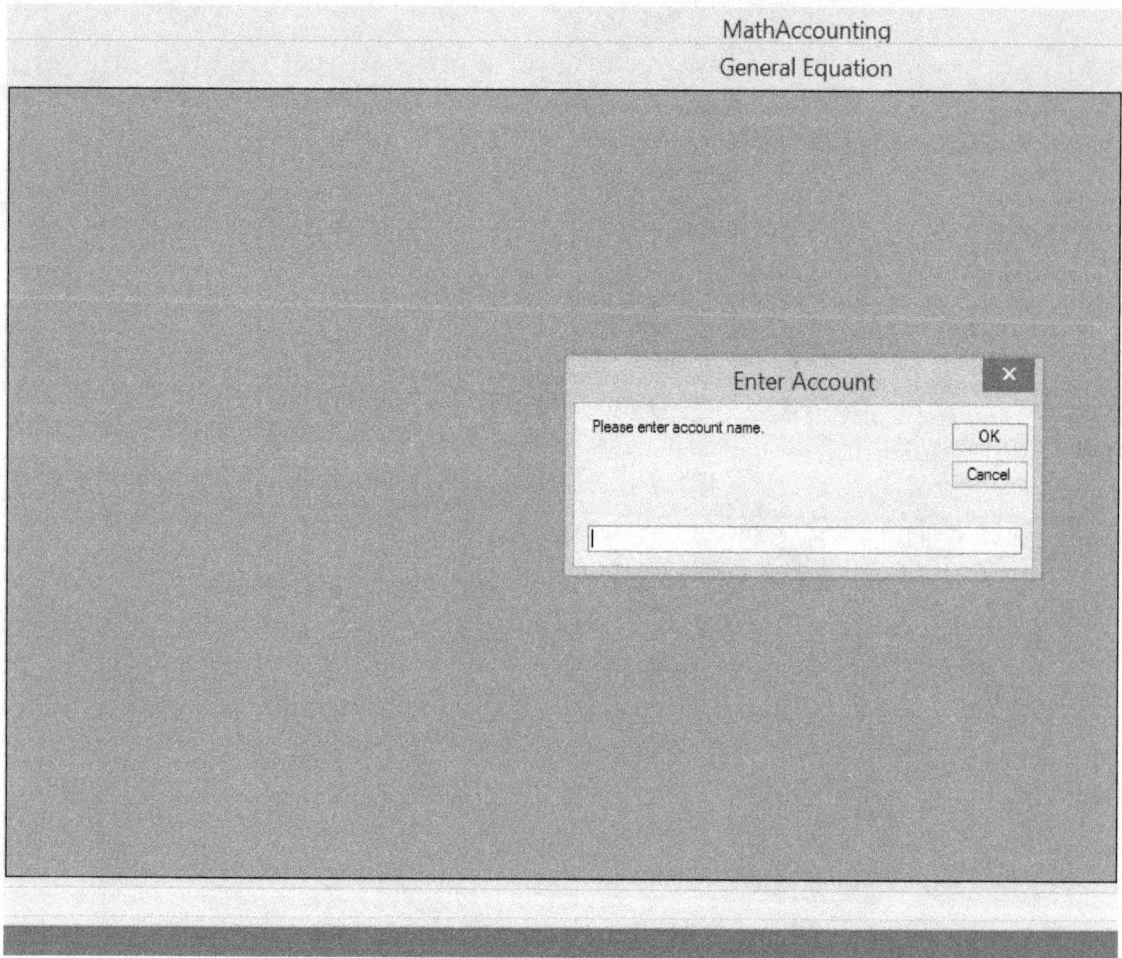

Figure 2-19   Entering Account Name

ID	Multi-Name	Amount	Balance	General ID	Transaction Date	Reference(Row)
1	Inven111<Inven11<Inven1	$1,650.00	$1,650.00	4	2014-01-05	
2	Inven112<Inven11<Inven1	$900.00	$2,550.00	4	2014-01-05	
3	Inven121<Inven12<Inven1	$520.00	$3,070.00	4	2014-01-05	
4	Inven122<Inven12<Inven1	$330.00	$3,400.00	4	2014-01-05	
5	Inven13<Inven1	$270.00	$3,670.00	4	2014-01-05	
6	Inven111<Inven11<Inven1	-$910.00	$2,760.00	5	2014-01-05	
7	Inven112<Inven11<Inven1	-$520.00	$2,240.00	5	2014-01-05	
8	Inven121<Inven12<Inven1	-$300.00	$1,940.00	5	2014-01-05	
9	Inven122<Inven12<Inven1	-$170.00	$1,770.00	5	2014-01-05	

Figure 2-20   Inventory Table

After clicking the EachSubAccount box and entering the "Inven122", I click the OK box and get the Figure 2-21on the next page.

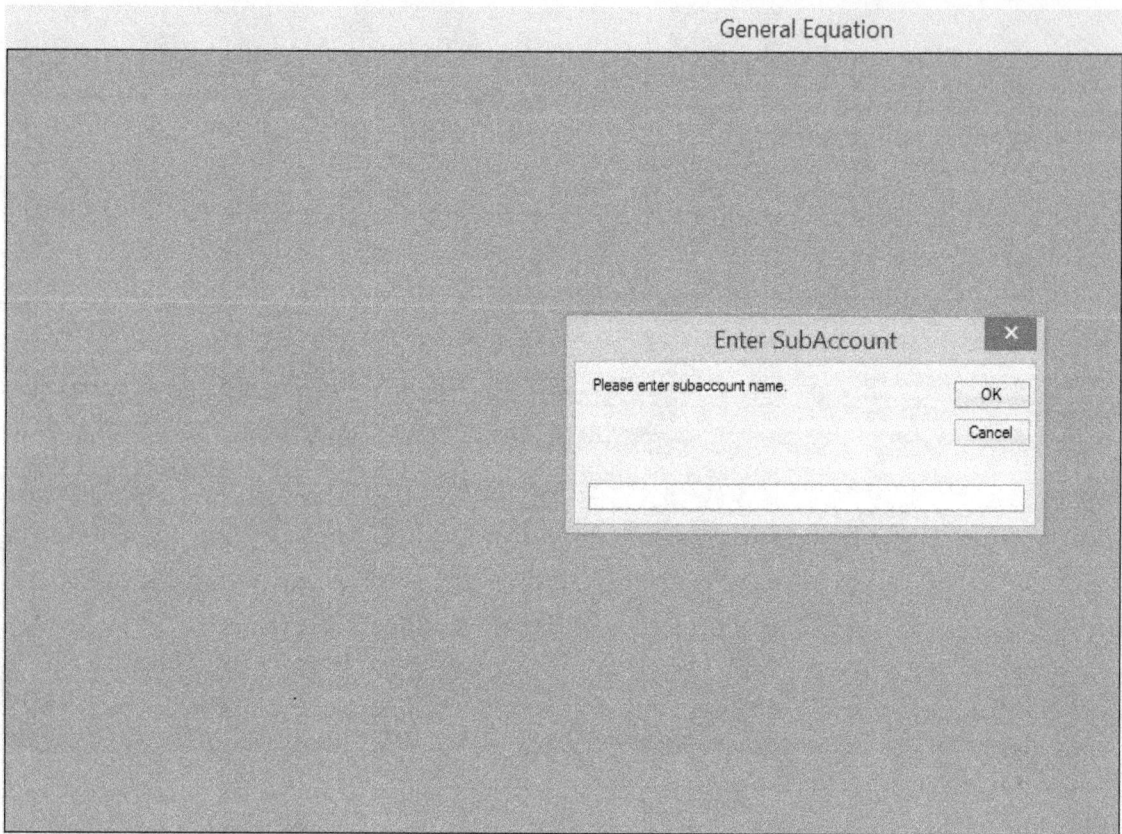

General Equation

Enter SubAccount

Please enter subaccount name.

OK

Cancel

Inventory: Inven122

	ID	Multi-Name	Amount	Reference	General ID	Transaction Date	Balance
▶	4	Inven122<Inven12<Inven1	$330.00		4	2014-01-05	
	9	Inven122<Inven12<Inven1	-$170.00		5	2014-01-05	
							$160.00
✱							

Figure 2-21   Three-Level Subaccount Inven122 Table

Now, we will take a look at the three boxes about the customers' information: Customers box, EachCustomer box, and AccoReceiAge box. Clicking the Customers box gets all customers' information. After clicking the EachCustomer box, I am required to enter this customer's telephone number. The Figure 2-22 on the next page shows the results after completing the steps correctly.

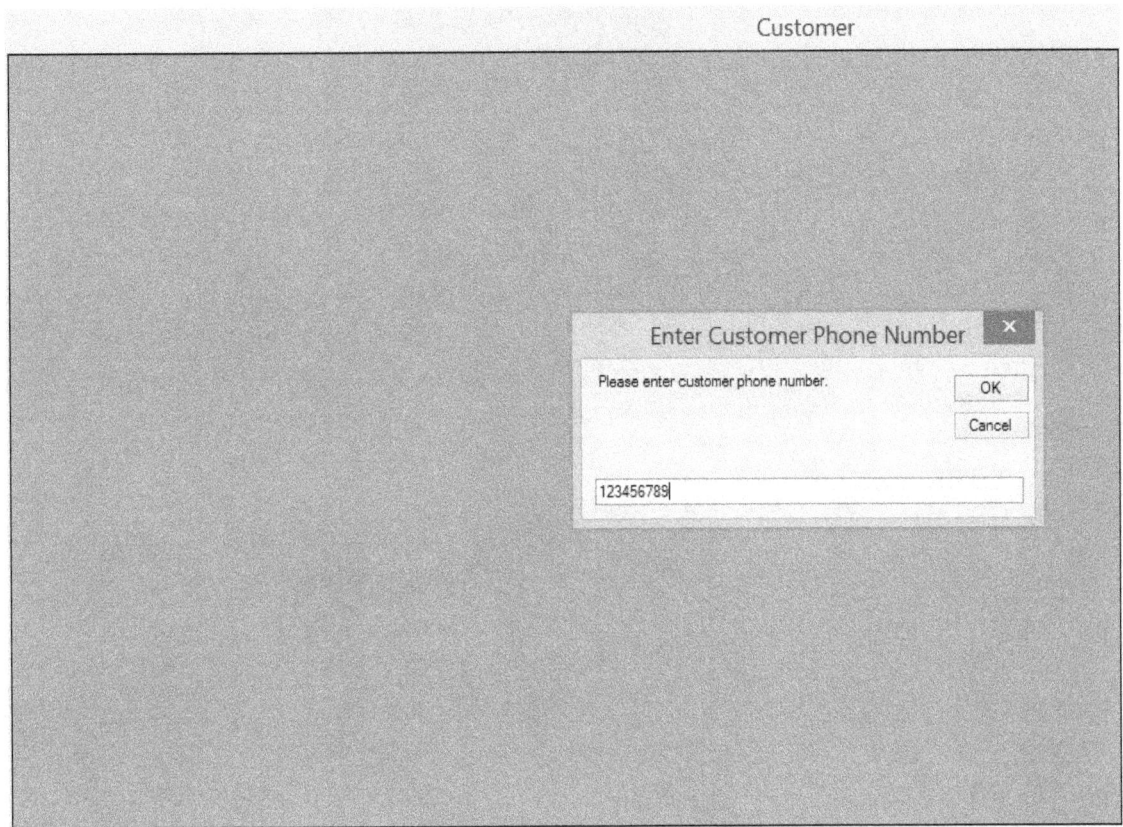

Figure 2-22   Account receivable for Customer B1

The AccoReceiAge box shows me how many customers and their balances there are in a special period, such as 30 days (account receivable age). After clicking this box and entering a period of 0-30, I get the Figure 2-23 from which there is not any number in the second table. Why? In fact, I have only entered one customer. Its account receivable age is greater than 30 days now.

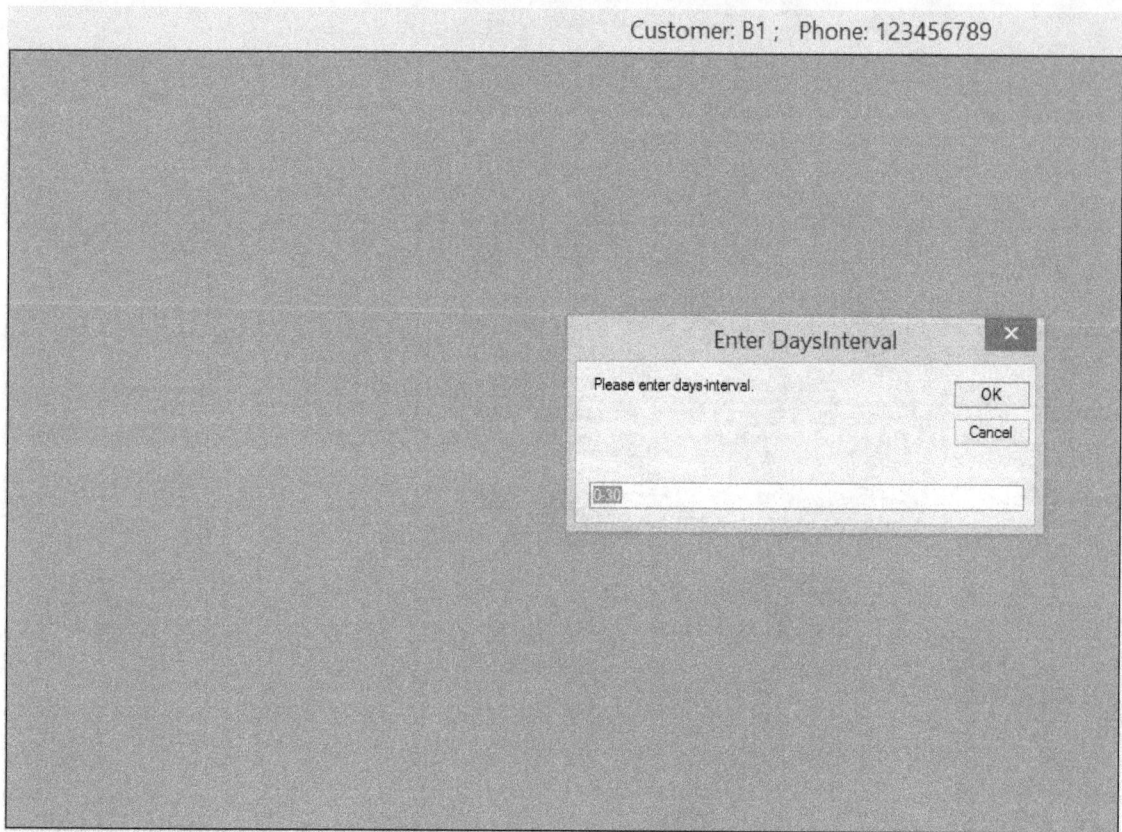

Customer: B1 ;   Phone: 123456789

Enter DaysInterval

Please enter days-interval.

OK

Cancel

0-30

Account Receivable Age of Every Customer

General ID	Amount	Day	Customer Name	Phone	Transaction Date	Balance
						$2,230.00

Figure 2-23   Every Customer's Account Receivable Age in period 0-30 days

Trying to enter a period of 800-900, I get the Figure 2-24 which tells me that there is one customer, its ages of day are 804 days, and its balance is $2,230.

Similar for the suppliers, I can get the information for every supplier.

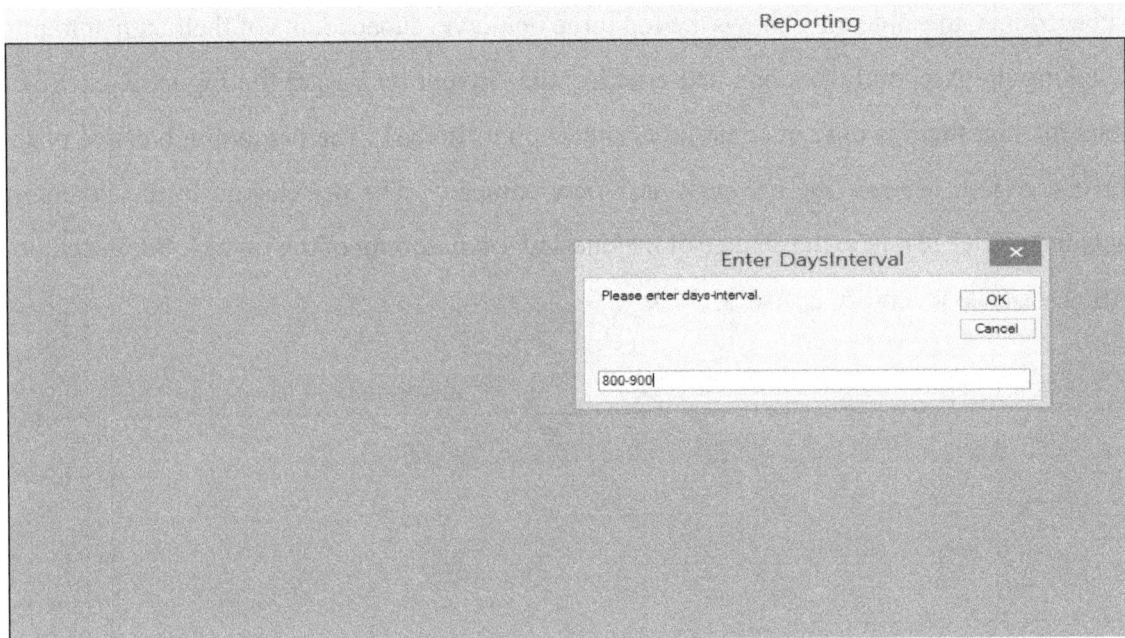

	General ID	Amount	Day	Customer Name	Phone	Transaction Date	Balance
▶	5	$2,230.00	804	B1	123456789	2014-01-05	
							$2,230.00
✳							

Figure 2-24   Every Customer's Account Receivable Age in period 800-900 days

The IncomeStatement, BalanceSheet, CashFlows, and ComprehensiveIncomeStatement boxes will be introduced later after entering more transactions. However, you can try to click them now.

The Reference, MultiSubaccount, and Subtotal Name boxes are the copies of the tables in the database which I entered the data into. You can try to click them to get the information.

I am interested in the AcountFlows box. After clicking this box, I get a table which is similar as the cash flows statement. When an account has more than three one-level subaccounts, the table only shows the top three one-level subaccounts of their sum amounts. Clicking the AccountFlows box and entering the "inventory", I get the Figure 2-25 which tells me that there is only one one-level subaccount: Inven1. The beginning balance of the inventory is 0 because the company is a new company. The net change in the inventory account is $1,770 due to the change of the one-level subaccount of the Inven1. So, the ending balance of the inventory is also $1,770.

Inventory Flows Statement	
Inventory Flows Statement Year Ended 2014-12-30	
Inven1	
Inven11	$1,120.00
Inven12	$380.00
Inven13	$270.00
Net Inventory provided by Inven1	$1,770.00
	$0.00
	$0.00
	$0.00
	$0.00
	$0.00
	$0.00
	$0.00
Net change in Inventory	$1,770.00
Inventory, Begining	$0.00
Inventory, Ending	$1,770.00
	$0.00
Total Inventory, Ending	$1,770.00

Figure 2-25   Inventory Flow Statement

2.3 Backup/Restore function model

The reliability and correctness of recording data in the accounting are very important, so I pay more attention to this subject in designing the MathAccounting software. There are three steps to guarantee the recording data reliable and correct.

- Check whether the dynamic accounting equation is equal.
- Check whether the sum of all assets accounts' balances is equal to the sum of all

liabilities accounts, all equity accounts, all incomes accounts, and all expenses accounts' balances.

- After the previous two steps are correct, I check whether the left (or right) amount of the dynamic accounting equation is equal to the sum of all assets accounts' balances (or the sum of all liabilities, all equity accounts, all incomes accounts, and all expenses accounts' balances).

After the above three conditions are all satisfied, the MathAccounting software can continue the next transaction's entries.

When I turn on computer to readily enter the new transactions, the computer automatically checks the three steps, which guarantees that the new transactions are entered into the reliable and correct database. If one of them is wrong, the computer will tell me that I must restore the previous day's database backup.

After I enter one day's transactions (or every transaction) and begin to do the backup of the database, the computer automatically also checks the three steps, which guarantees the backup of the database is reliable and correct. If one of them is wrong, I cannot do the backup of the just renewed database. I must find the mistakes during today's entries and correct the mistakes or I should restore the previous day's backup and begin today's transactions (or every transaction) again. Do not worry about that. The situation seldom appears because every entry of the transactions is required to check the sub-equation. Maybe, the breakdown of the computer can cause the trouble during entering a transaction.

Clicking the Backup/Restore box, I get the Figure 2-26, seeing the next page. The Figure 2-26 has six boxes. The three boxes of the first row are every day backup, every month backup, and one year backup before beginning the new fiscal year.

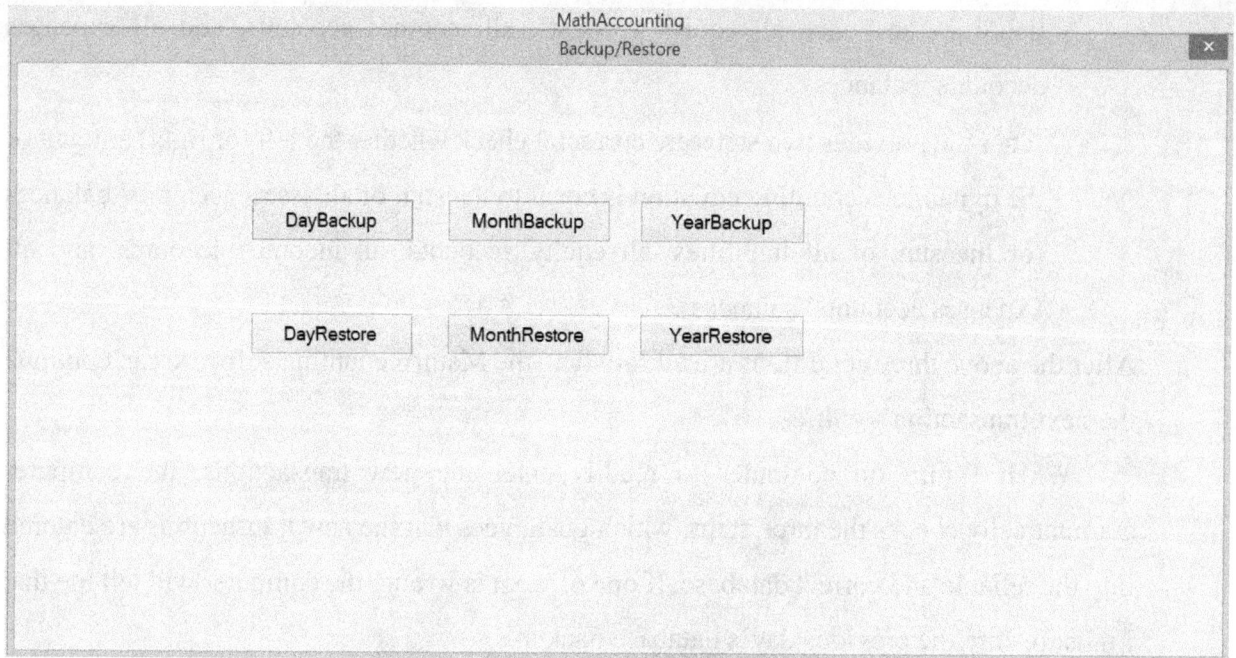

Figure 2-26   Backup/Restore Interface

The DayBackup means that the today's entries of all transactions are added up to the existing backup database. Of course, I can also use the DayBackup box to do every transaction's backup. After clicking the DayBackup box and the OK box, I get the Figure 2-27, seeing the next page. Clicking the OK box again, I have completed the DayBackup.

The MonthBackup is the same as the DayBack.

The YearBackup is different. You can do the YearBackup only after you complete the income statement.

| DayBackup | MonthBackup | YearBackup |

| DayRestore | M |

General Equation: 13583.0000 = 13583.0000

OK

| DayBackup | MonthBackup | YearBackup |

| DayRestore | Mo | re |

All accounts: 13583.0000 = 13583.0000

OK

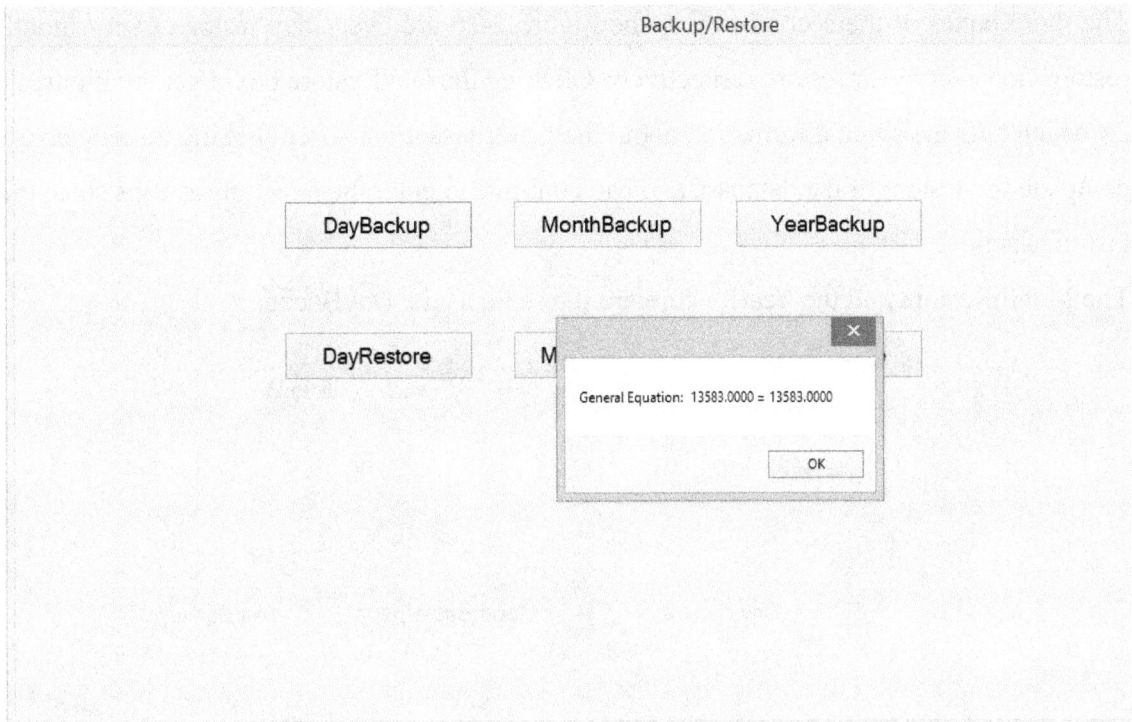

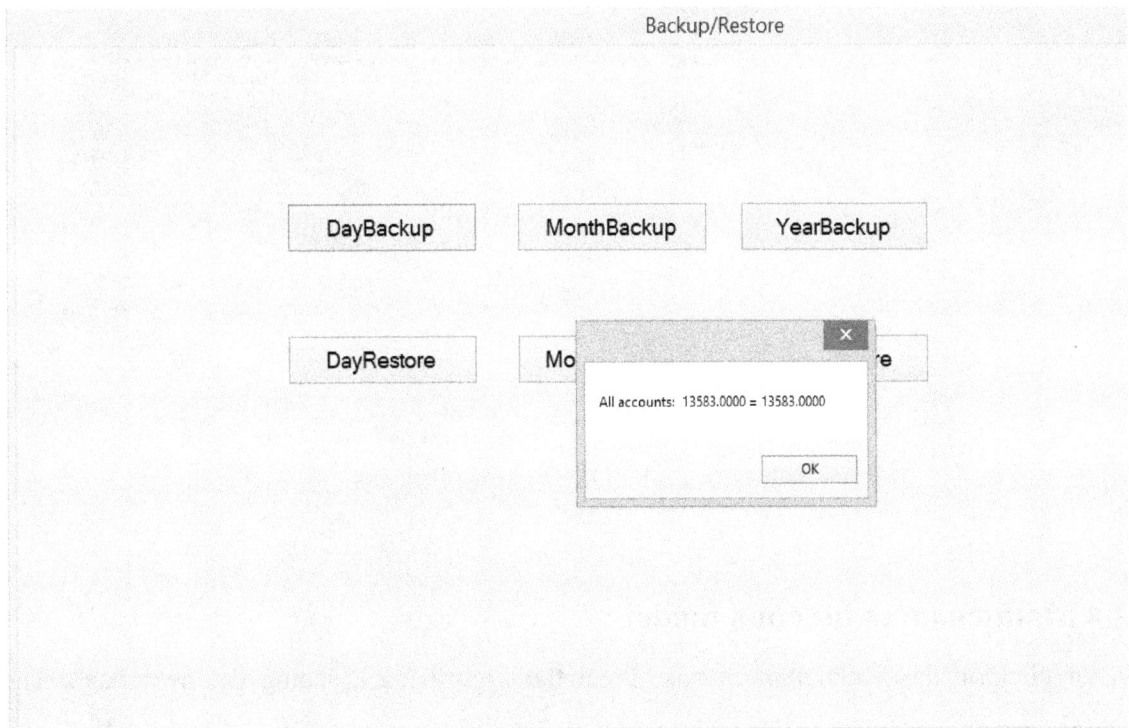

Figure 2-27   Day Backup Process

The three boxes of the second row in the Figure 2-26 are every day restore, every month restore, and every year restore respectively. Clicking the DayRestore box, I get the Figure 2-28 which tells me some information about the last transaction. After clicking the OK box, I complete the restore of the database and can continue to enter the new transactions since the last transaction.

The MonthRestore and the YearRestore are the same as the DayBackup.

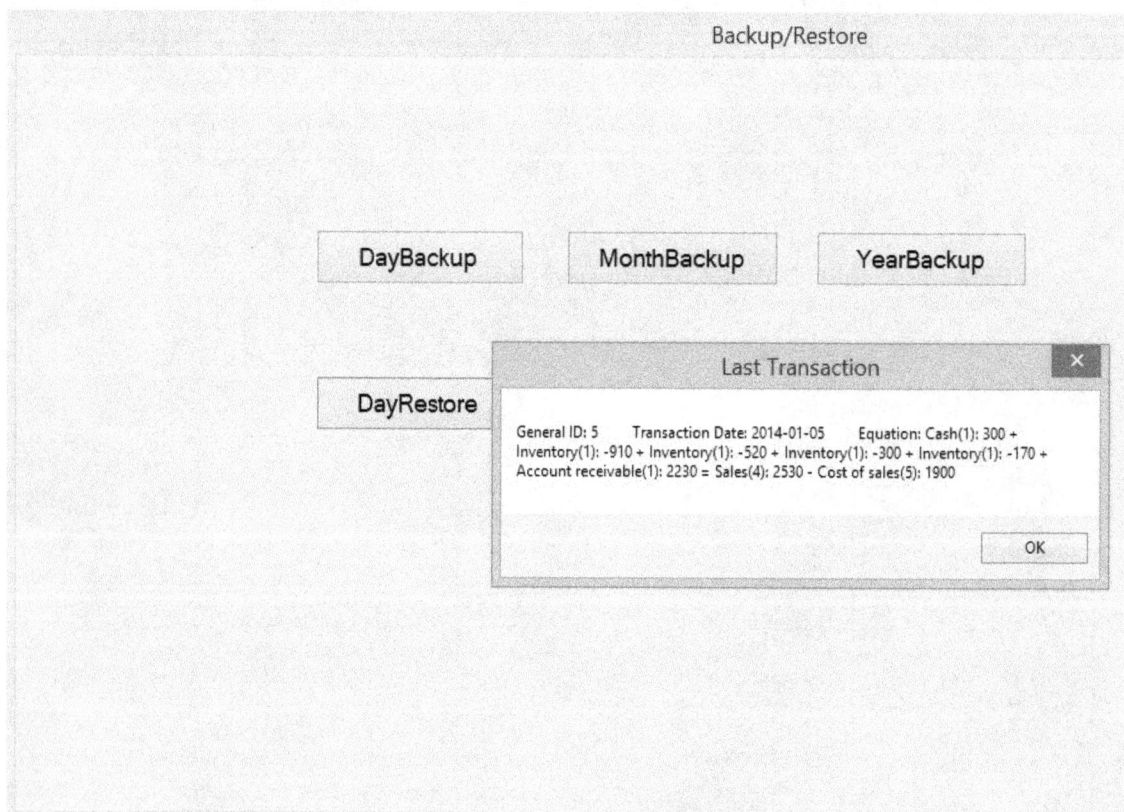

Figure 2-28   Day Restore Process

2.4 Maintenances function model

After clicking the Maintenances box, I get the Figure 2-29, seeing the next page. The maintenances function model is mainly used to alter parent account names, multi-subaccount name, and subtotal name, and delete the useless parent account names.

AlteringAccountNames	AlteringMultiSubaccountName
DeletingAccountNames	AlteringSubtotalName

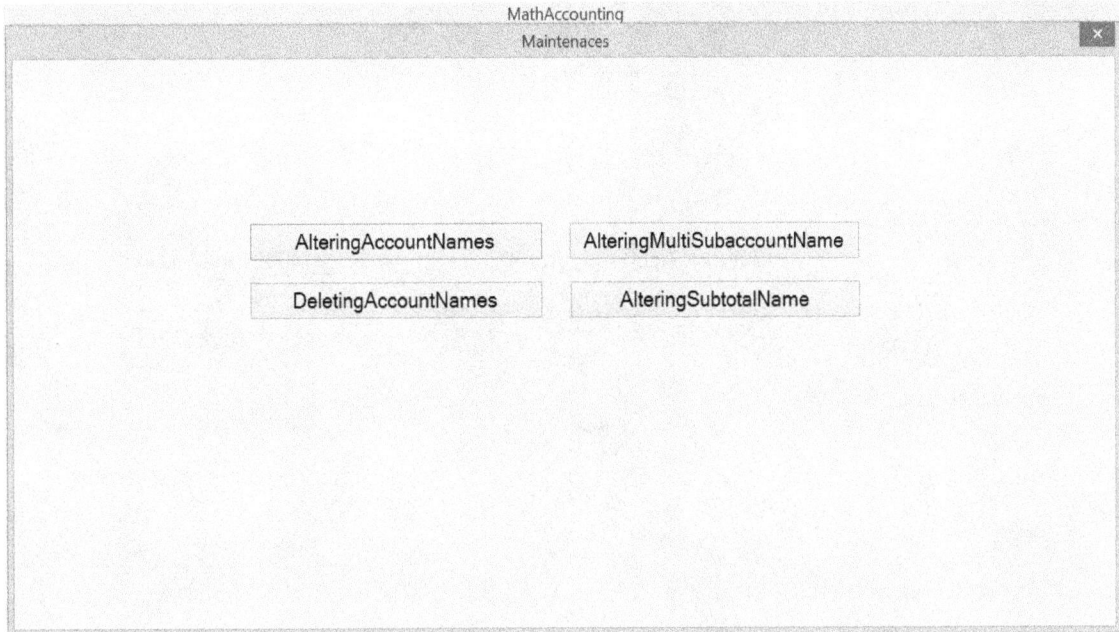

Figure 2-29   Maintenances Function Model Interface

If I want to change the "Supplies" account to the "Office supplies" account, then I can click the AlteringAccountName box to do that. However, if I want to put the new account of the "Office supplies" under the account of the "Inventory" at same time (now the "Supplies" account is above the "Inventory" account), then I can only do that by use of clicking the DeletingAccountName box. First, I delete the account of the "Supplies", and then I can build a new account of "Office supplies" which is under the account of the "Inventory" by entering correct row number in the Transaction function model.

After clicking the AlteringAccountName box, entering old account name, pressing the OK box, and entering the new account name, I get the Figure 2-30, seeing the next page. Simply pressing the OK box again, I have changed the "Supplies" account to the "Office supplies" account.

AlteringAccountNames   AlterinqMultiSubaccountName

DeletingAcc

Enter OLD Account   ×

Please enter OLD account name.   OK

Cancel

otalName

supplier

Altering Account Name

AlteringAccountNames   AlterinqMultiSubaccountName

DeletingAcc

Enter NEW Account   ×

Please enter NEW account name.   OK

Cancel

otalName

Office supplies

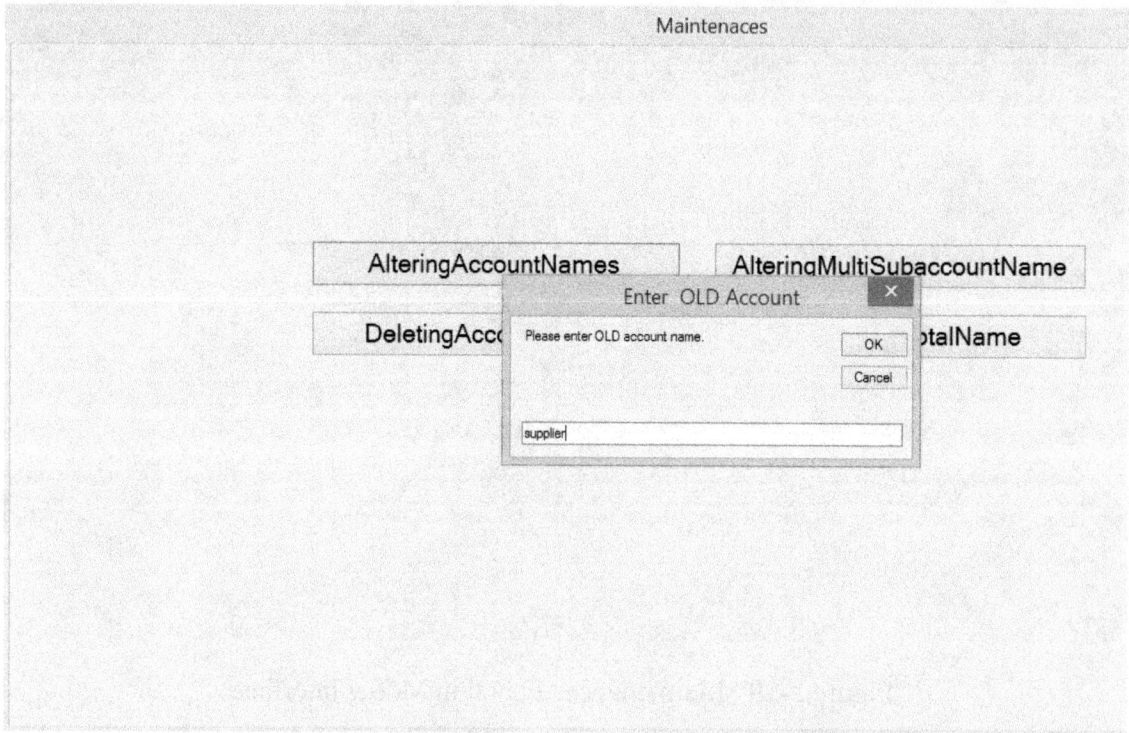

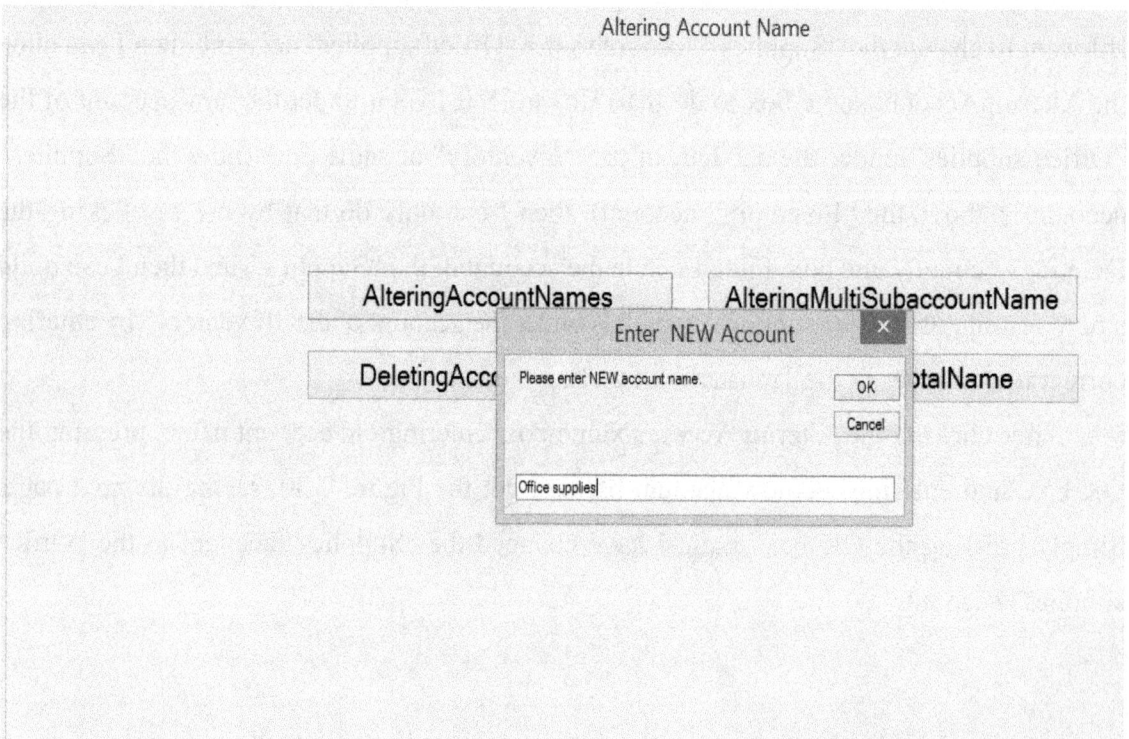

Figure 2-30   Altering Account Name

If there is a mistake that the Inven13 does not belong to the Inven1 and belongs to the Inven2 in previous entries, then I must replace the multi-subaccount name of the "Inven13<Inven1" with the multi-subaccount name of the "Inven21<Inven2". Clicking the AlteringMultiSubaccountName box, entering old multi-subaccount name, pressing OK box, and entering the new multi-subaccount name, I get the Figure 2-31. Simply pressing the OK box again, I have changed the multi-subaccount name of the "Inven13<Inven1" to the "Inven21<Inven2".

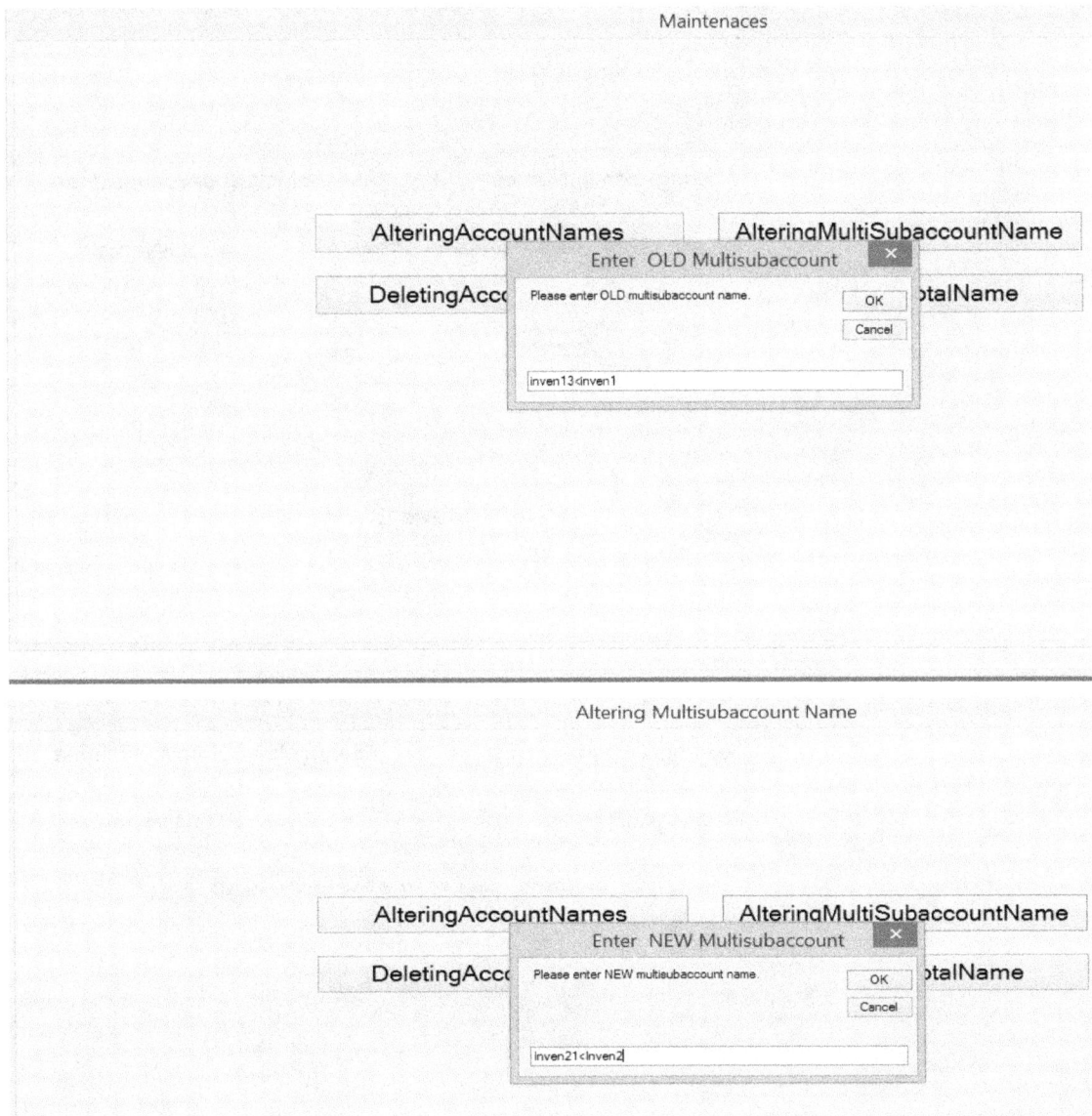

Maintenaces

| AlteringAccountNames | AlteringMultiSubaccountName |

Enter OLD Multisubaccount ×

DeletingAcc   Please enter OLD multisubaccount name.   OK   otalName

Cancel

inven13<inven1

Altering Multisubaccount Name

| AlteringAccountNames | AlteringMultiSubaccountName |

Enter NEW Multisubaccount ×

DeletingAcc   Please enter NEW multisubaccount name.   OK   otalName

Cancel

inven21<Inven2

Figure 2-31   Altering Multisubaccount Name

Similar as the MultiSubaccount name, I can change the subtotal name by clicking the Subtotal Name box. However, I must emphasize that the row number of the subtotal name is not allowed to change because there may be many accounts under this subtotal name.

If the account of the "Office supplies" is useless, I can delete the account by clicking the DeletingAccountName. When I enter the account name and press the OK box, I get warning information, seeing the Figure 2-32.

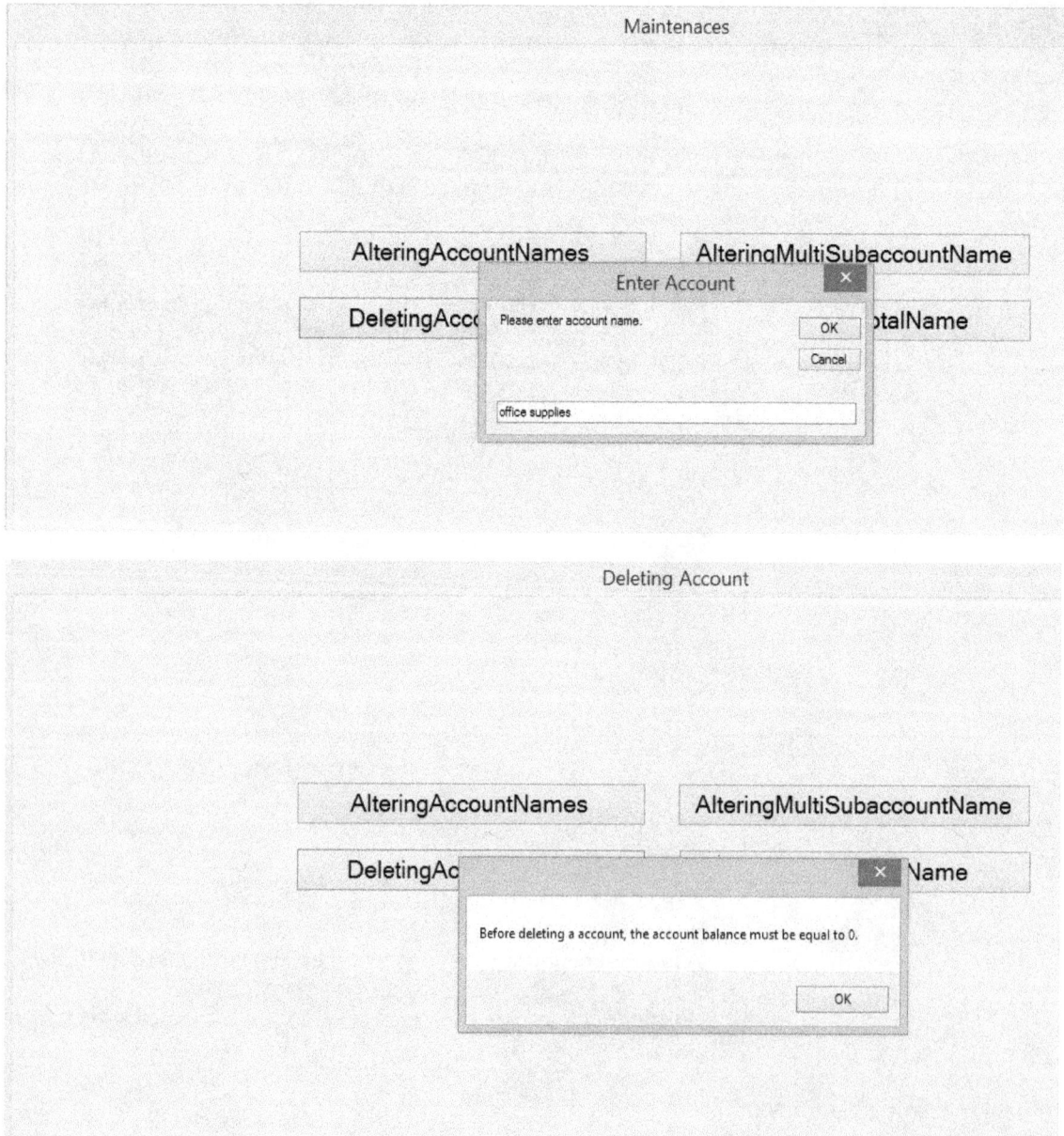

Figure 2-32   Warning before Deleting an Account

The account balance must be 0, so I enter the following transaction in the Transaction function model before deleting the "Office supplies" account.

Office supplies (1) -193 = - Office expenses (5) 193

Clicking the DeletingAccountName box again and press the OK box, I have deleted the account of the "Office supplies".

Now I can check these changes. Closing the Maintenances function model and opening the Reports function model. After respectively clicking the TotalAccount box for assets and expenses, and the Multi-subaccount Name box, I can get the Figure 2-33, seeing this page and the next page. From the Figure 2-33, these changes have been done. The account of the "Office supplies" disappears from the asset table, and the account of the "Office expenses" appears in expenses table. The "Inven21<Inven2" has replaced the "Inven13<Inven1".

That is all of the MathAccounting software. It is easy?

	Asset		
Name	Subtotal	Balance
▸ Account receivable	Current assests,103	$2,230.00
Cash	Current assests,103	$9,390.00
Inventory	Current assests,103	$1,770.00
＊		

Figure 2-33   Check These Changes (Continue)

Expense

Name	Subtotal	Balance
Cost of sales	Cost,431	$1,900.00
Office expenses	Operating and administrative expens...	$193.00
Travelling expenses	Operating and administrative expens...	$47.00

MultiSubaccount Name

Class	Account Name	MultiSubaccount Name	ID
1	Cash	Cash receipts from owners<Financing activities	1
1	Cash	Cash payment to suppliers<Operating activities	8
1	Inventory	Inven111<inven11<Inven1	9
1	Inventory	Inven112<Inven11<Inven1	10
1	Inventory	Inven121<Inven12<Inven1	11
1	Inventory	Inven122<Inven12<Inven1	12
1	Inventory	Inven21<Inven2	13
1	Cash	Cash payment for operating expenses<Operating activities	5
1	Supplies	n	6
1	Cash	Cash receipts from customers<Operating activities	15
1	Account receivable	123456789	16
2	Account payable	987654321	14
3	Share capital	Capital-Ping Wang	2
3	Share capital	Capital-Hua Li	3
3	Share capital	Capital-Mike Newsome	4
4	Sales	Xiao Zhou-Sales	17
5	Travelling	Hua Li-Travelling<Department-Travelling	7

Figure 2-33   Check These Changes

In addition, the functions of the human resource and inventory management have been developed in the MathAccounting Software. If all subaccounts (including one-level subaccounts of factories, two-level subaccounts of departments, and three-level subaccounts of employees' ID) of the parent account "Salary Expenses" and all one-level subaccounts (Net Payroll Payable, tax Payable, and so on) of the parent account "Salary Payable" are designed to have 9,999 subaccounts, then human resource department can also use the MathAccounting Software to deal with work of the human resource management. In the chapter 5, I will introduce the human resource management in detail. The inventory management is similar to the human resource management. However, while entering inventory amount, its form is the "unit price*number".

In the two function models, the "cash" account cannot been used. Instead, the account of the "Something payable" is used.

Chapter 3

Sample of an accounting fiscal year

Last thing is to enter more transactions to complete an accounting fiscal year. During entering these transactions, I will introduce some new contents. Finally, I will build the five tables: Income Statement, Balance Sheet, Cash Flows Statement, Comprehensive Income Statement, and Account Flows Statement, and begin second fiscal year.

3.1 First fiscal year

First, I restoring the backup of the database data just with the previous five transactions, and change the multi-subaccount name of the "Inven13<Inven1" to the "Inven21<Inven2" again. Later I will build the multi-subaccount name of the "Inven13<Inven1" if purchasing them.

- RR Company raises funds of $500,000 cash with interest rate 8% (paying interest at the end of each year) and two years from TD bank on January 7, 2014.

  For the first entry of the "Cash" account, the Multisubaccount Name box is the "Cash receipts from banks< Financing activities". For the second entry of the "Note payable", the Subtotal Name box is the "Long term liabilities, 251"; the Multisubaccount Name box is "n" because it has not any subaccount.

- On same day, RR Company purchases two lands (Land1, Downtown for $270,000; Land2, North York for $180,000) for $450,000 cash as available for sale.

  For first entry of the "Cash" account, the Multisubaccount Name box is the "Cash payments for investment<Investing activities".

  For the entry of the "Land" account with two one-level subaccounts, the Subtotal Name box is the "Long term investments,141" and the Multisubaccount

Name box are the "Land1, Downtown" and "Land2, North York".

- On January 8, 2014, RR Company purchases a truck for $45,000 cash.

    For first entry of the "Cash" account, the Multisubaccount Name box is the "Cash payments to machinery<Operating activities". For second entry of the "Truck" account, the Multisubaccount Name box is "n" because it has not any subaccount, and the Subtotal Name box is the "Equipments, 171".

- On the same day, RR Company pays $367 cash to Ping Wang (Office department) for opening company expenses.

    Here, I put the expenses into the "Other expenses" account which has the two-level subaccounts and is divided by the different persons and the different departments. The "Other expenses" account is under the "Travelling expenses" account, so it may have the row number of the "456".

    Please pay attention here. Because the "Travelling expenses" account is also divided by the different persons and the different departments, I must give a different multi-subaccount name to distinguish them. Its multi-subaccount form is the "Ping Wang-other<Office department-other". Of course, you can give your distinguishing signal.

- On January 9, 2014, RR Company purchases $25,000 inventory for $2,000 cash and $23,000 on credit from C1 Company (phone number: 987654322).

    The inventory's multi-subaccounts are:

    "Inven221<Inven22<Inven2" for $10*320,

    "Inven222<Inven22< Inven2" for $5*1000,

    "PPUK parts <ASD parts< Inven2" for $4*1200,

    "PPGH parts <ASD parts< Inven2" for $2*1900,

    "Inven31<Inven3" for$ 10*530,

    "Inven32<Inven3" for $5*580.

- On same day, RR Company purchases $12,000 inventory on credit from D1 Company (phone number: 987654323).

    The inventory's multi-subaccounts are:

"Inven331<Inven33<Inven3" for $2*1350,

"Inven332<Inven33< Inven3" for $5*620,

"HGFCVB parts<QASXC parts<Inven3" for $10*490,

"PPGHUP parts<ASDUP parts<Inven3" for $10*130.

- On January 11, 2014, Xiao Zhou sales $17,700 inventory for $3,500 cash and $26,000 on credit to E1 Company (phone number: 123456788).

  The inventory's multi-subaccounts are:

  "Inven221<Inven22<Inven2" of cost $-10*290,

  "Inven222<Inven22<Inven2" of cost $-5*940,

  "PPUK parts<ASD parts< Inven2" of cost $-4*650,

  "Inven32<Inven3" of cost $-5*380,

  "HGFCVB parts<QASXC parts<Inven3" of cost $-10*480,

  "PPGHUP parts<ASDUP parts<Inven3" of cost -$10*80.

  Because the entries number of this transaction are greater than eight, I must divide the transaction into two transactions: one transaction for Inven2 sales and another transaction for Inven3 sales, or one transaction for cash, account receivable, and sales, and another for inventory and cost of sales. Here, I use the second method to divide this transaction. The two sub-equations are:

  Cash (1): 3500 + Account receivable (1): 26000 = Sales (4): 29500

  Inventory (1): -17700 = -Cost of sales (5): 17700

- On January 15, 2014, ZhenDao Yuan sales $13,200 inventory for $21,700 on credit to F1 Company (phone number: 123456787).

  The inventory's multi-subaccounts are:

  "PPGH parts<ASD parts<Inven2" of cost $-2*1550,

  "Inven31<Inven3" of cost $-10*500,

  "Inven331<Inven33<Inven3" of cost $-2*1100,

  "Inven332<Inven33< Inven3" of cost $-5*580.

- On January 17, 2014, RR Company purchases $12,500 inventory on credit from G1 Company (phone number: 987654324).

  The inventory's multi-subaccounts are:

  "Inven411<Inven41<Inven4" for $5*1020,

  "Inven412<Inven41<Inven4" for $2*1850,

  "TTTCU parts<TTT parts<Inven4" for $2*1150,

  "RRRHJK parts< Inven4" for $ 2*700.

- On the same day, RR Company receives $21,000 cash from E1 Company (phone number: 123456788) with the General ID 12.

  Please pay attention, the General ID 12 must be the General ID of the transaction including the "Account receivable" account because the previous transaction is divided into two transactions.

  Entering an existed customer's phone number gets the Figure 3-1, seeing the next page. From the Figure 3-1, the Reference box is enabled while entering the phone number. The "Account receivable" account is not a new account, so I do not need to enter a row number. Why? Here, you must pay an attention for that. In fact, when I receive the $21000 cash, I know that E1 Company pays the cash. However, the computer does not know that, so I must tell the computer which customer pays the cash. I borrow the Reference box to enter the General ID of the previous related transaction. This General ID can be gotten from the general equation table, or each customer's table, or account receivable table and is 12.

  Maybe you ask why I do not use the customer' phone number as the judging signal. Because a company may sale the inventory to this customer for a few of times and the General ID of a transaction is sole, I must choose the General ID as the judging signal. The Figure 3-2, which follows the Figure 3-1, shows the relationship between the ID 2 transaction with the General ID 12 and the ID 4 transaction with the Reference 12 in the two tables of the account receivable and the customer.

Transaction

Assets(1) = Liabilities(2) + Equity(3) + Incomes(4) - Expenses(5)

1/17/2014	any (phone number: 123456788)	1	Account receivable ˅	-21000	123456788	˅
Trans date	Explanation	Class	Account Name	Amount	MultiSubaccount Name	

[˅] [˅]
Reference

No.	TransDate	Class	Account Name	MultiSubaccount Name	Amouunt	
2	1/17/2014	1	Cash	Cash receipts from customers<Operating activities	21000	Continue

---

Transaction

Assets(1) = Liabilities(2) + Equity(3) + Incomes(4) - Expenses(5)

1/17/2014	any (phone number: 123456788)	1	Account receivable ˅	-21000	123456788	˅
Trans date	Explanation	Class	Account Name	Amount	MultiSubaccount Name	

[˅] [12 ˅]
Reference

No.	TransDate	Class	Account Name	MultiSubaccount Name	Amouunt	
2	1/17/2014	1	Cash	Cash receipts from customers<Operating activities	21000	Continue

Figure 3-1   Reference Box's other use

MathAccounting

Account receivable

	ID	Multi-Name	Amount	Balance	General ID	Transaction Date	Reference(Row)
▶	1	123456789	$2,230.00	$2,230.00	5	2014-01-05	110
	2	123456788	$26,000.00	$28,230.00	12	2014-01-11	
	3	123456787	$21,700.00	$49,930.00	14	2014-01-15	
	4	123456788	-$21,000.00	$28,930.00	17	2014-01-17	12
*							

MathAccounting

Customer: E1 ;   Phone: 123456788

	ID	Amount	Reference	Genera ID	Transaction Date
▶	2	$26,000.00		12	2014-01-11
	4	-$21,000.00	12	16	2014-01-17
		$5,000.00			
*					

Figure 3-2   Relationships between General ID 12 and General ID 16

- On January 21, 2014, RR Company pays $14,000 cash to C1 Company (phone number: 987654322) with the General ID 10.

  The same thing is for the suppliers about the Reference box.

- On same day, RR Company pays $6,000 cash to D1 Company (phone number: 987654323) with the General ID 11.

- On January 22, 2014, RR Company purchases $21,500 inventory on credit from C1 Company (phone number: 987654322).

  The inventory's multi-subaccounts are:

  "PPUK parts<ASD parts<Inven2" for $4*1625,

  "PPGH parts<ASD parts<Inven2" for $2*3000,

  "Inven31<Inven3" for$ 10*530,

  "Inven32<Inven3" for $5*740.

- On January 23, 2014, Yi Liu sales $12,000 inventory for $19,900 on credit to F1 Company (phone number: 123456787).

  The inventory's multi-subaccounts are:

  "PPUK parts<ASD parts<Inven2" of cost $-4*825,

  "PPGH parts<ASD parts<Inven2" of cost $-2*1950,

  "Inven31<Inven3" of cost $-10*250,

  "Inven32<Inven3" of cost $-5*460.

- On January 25, 2014, ZhenDao Yuan sales $7,500 inventory for $13,700 on credit to H1 Company (phone number: 123456786).

  The inventory's multi-subaccounts are:

  "PPUK parts<ASD parts<Inven2" of cost $-4*750,

  "PPGH parts<ASD parts<Inven2" of cost $-2*900,

  "Inven31<Inven3" of cost $-10*270.

- On January 28, 2014, RR Company purchases $5,600 computers equipment for $5,600 cash.

  The computer account has three one-level subaccounts of the computer1 ($1,600), the computer server ($1,800), and the POS system ($2,200). It belongs to the Subtotal of the "Equipments".

- On January 29, 2014, Jun Wang sales $3,500 inventory for $6,200 on credit to B1 Company (phone number: 123456789).

The inventory's multi-subaccounts are:

"PPUK parts<ASD parts<Inven2" of cost $-4*550,

"Inven32<Inven3" of cost $-5*260.

- On January 30, 2014, RR Company receives $2,000 cash from B1 Company (phone number: 123456789) with the General ID 5.

- On the same day, RR Company receives $15,000 cash from F1 Company (phone number: 123456787) with the General ID 14.

- On the same day, RR Company receives $8,000 cash from H1 Company (phone number: 123456786) with the General ID 23.

- On the same day, RR Company pays $7,000 cash to C1Company (phone number: 987654322) with the General ID 10.

- On the same day, RR Company pays $232.76 cash to Dan Zhu (Purchase department) for the travelling expenses $178 and the other expenses $54.76.

- On the same day, RR Company pays $221.30 cash to Hua Li (Purchase department) for the travelling expenses $135.12 and the other expenses $86.18.

- On the same day, RR Company pays $339.52 cash to Xiao Zhou (Sales department) for the travelling expenses $243 and the other expenses $96.52.

- On the same day, RR Company pays $132.26 cash to Jun Wang (Sales department) for the other expenses.

- On the same day, RR Company pays $82.33 cash to Zhendao Yuan (Sales department) for the other expenses.

- On January 31, 2014, RR Company receives $13,000 cash from F1Company (phone number: 123456787) with the General ID 22.

- On the same day, RR Company pays $8,000 cash to G1Company (phone number: 987654324) with the General ID 15.

- On the same day, RR Company pays $419.55 cash to Yi Liu (Sales department) for the travelling expenses $347.7 and the other expenses $71.85.

- On the same day, RR Company records the office supplies expenses $88.

- On the same day, RR Company pays $18,756 cash for all salary of January, 2014.

Here, I just consider the total salary and have no detail of the payments. I will introduce the human resource function later.

- On the same day, RR Company records the truck's amortization expenses $750 one month (5 years, straight line, and full first month).

  The "Amortization expenses" account is a parent account which will appear in the income statement. It has a one-level subaccount "Truck-amortization" now.

  The "Accumulated amortization" is a contra account of the "Truck" account, so I should reverse the amount of the contra account while putting the contra account into the class 1 accounts. The reversing amount means that increasing amount is the "-" and decreasing amount is the "+". The "Accumulated amortization" should be under the "Truck" parent account whose row number is the "172", so its row number should be the "173". Because the contra account "Accumulated amortization: truck" will also appear in the financial statements, it seems a parent account and has a one-level subaccount "Truck-accumulated amortization" now.

  There are other contra accounts too, such as the "Allowance for doubtful account" for the "Account receivable" account and the "Discount on bonds payable" for the "Bonds payable" account. The same method can be used for them.

- On the same day, RR Company records the computers' amortization expenses $101.39.

  The "Amortization expenses" account has two one-level subaccounts of the "Truck-amortization and Computer-amortization" now. The "Computers" account has three one-level subaccounts of the computer1 (two years, straight line, and half first month of $33.33), the computer server (two years, straight line, and half first month of $37.5), and the POS system (three years, straight line, and half first month of $30.56). Therefore, for the "Computer" account, its "Amortization expenses" account should have three two-level subaccounts. Their multi-subaccounts are:

  "Computer1- amortization< Computer - amortization",

  "Computer server - amortization< Computer - amortization",

  "POS system - amortization< Computer - amortization".

The parent account of the "Accumulated amortization: Computer" should be under the parent account "Computer" whose row number is the "174", so its row number should be the "175". It has three one-level subaccounts which are also the multi-subaccounts:

Computer1- accumulated amortization

Computer server- accumulated amortization

POS system- accumulated amortization

- On the same day, RR Company pays $376.47 cash to Mike Newsome (Office department) for travelling expenses $298.69 and the other expenses $77.78.

- On the same day, RR Company pays $280.70 cash for the utility expenses.

- On the same day, RR Company pays $1500 cash for the office rent expenses.

- On the same day, RR Company records the note payable's interest expenses $3,000 and the accrued interest payable (500,000*8%/12*27/30).

I have completed the first month transactions so far. The same things basically are repeated in the following months. Now I can take a glance of the income statement, balance sheet, cash flows statement, and account flows statement. After clicking the IncomeStatement box and entering the ended date of the "1/31/2014" and the tax rate of the "0.3", I get the Figure 3-3 which shows that the net earnings is $7,725.

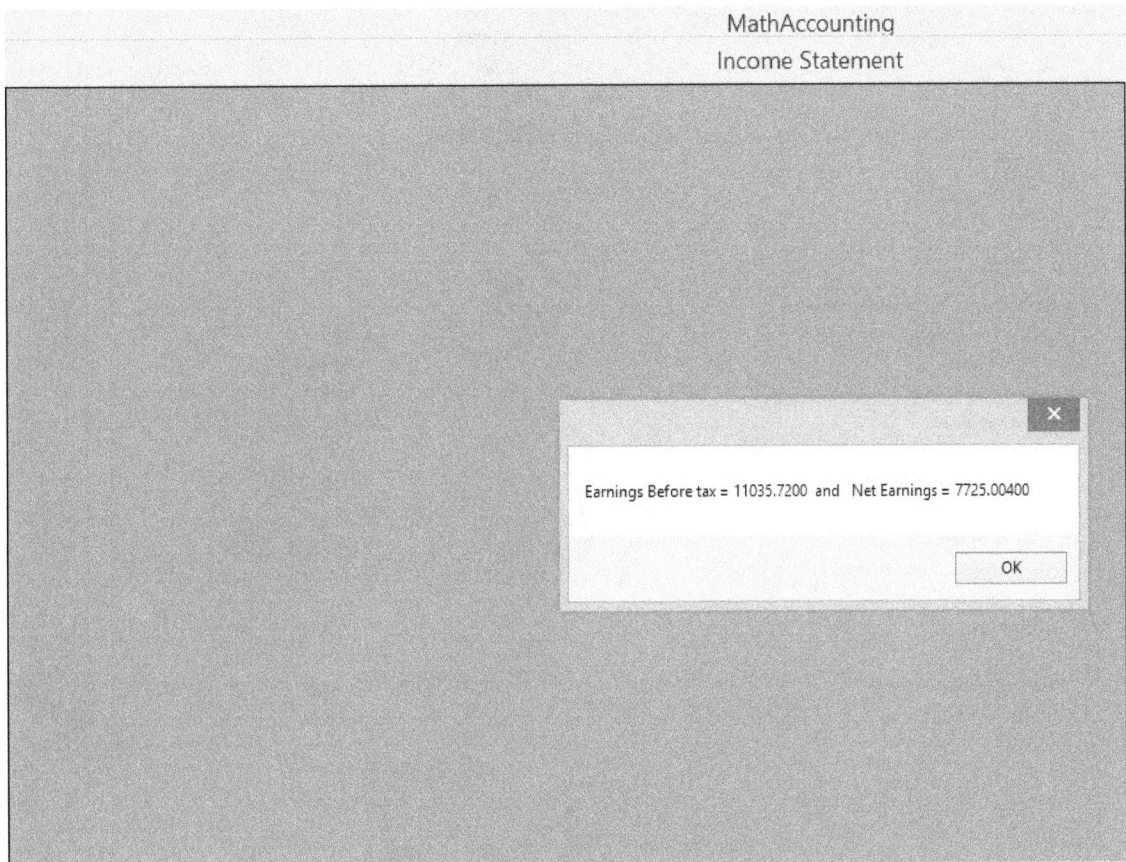

Earnings Before tax = 11035.7200 and Net Earnings = 7725.00400

Figure 3-3   Getting Net Income

Pressing OK box in the Figure 3-3 and answering the "No" for the question of the "Would you like to begin new fiscal year?" in the appearing information box, I get the income statement table, seeing the Figure 3-4. The row under the "Earnings before Income Taxes" are empty and the net earnings are $11,035.72. I do not enter the tax expenses which is $3,310.72 ($11,035.72-$7,725 = $3,310.72) into database and begin a new fiscal year, and the Reports function model does not check anything just as said before, so there is not the tax expenses row under the "Earnings Before Income Taxes" and the net earnings is $11,035.72.

MathAccounting		
Income Statement		

Year ended: 1/31/2014	
Revenues	
Sales	$93,530.00
Cost	
Cost of sales	-$55,800.00
Gross Margin	$37,730.00
Operating and administrative expenses	
Travelling expenses	-$1,249.51
Other expenses	-$968.68
Supplies expenses	-$88.00
Salary expenses	-$18,756.00
Amortization expenses	-$851.39
Utility expenses	-$280.70
Rent expenses	-$1,500.00
Interest expenses	-$3,000.00
Earnings Before Income Taxes	$11,035.72
Net Earnings	$11,035.72
Retained Earnings,Begining	$0.00
Retained Earnings,Ending	$11,035.72

Figure 3-4   Income Statement without Including Tax expenses

Clicking the BalanceSheet box gets the Figure 3-5, seeing the next page. The Figure 3-5 shows the balance sheet table. The total assets are $561,035.72, and the total liabilities and shareholders' equity are $550,000. Their difference is $11,035.72. The reason is the same as the income statements.

MathAccounting	
Balance Sheet	

As at 1/31/2014	
ASSETS	
Current assets	
Cash	$11,582.11
Supplies	$105.00
Inventory	$18,870.00
Account receivable	$30,730.00
	$61,287.11
Long term investments	
Land	$450,000.00
Equipments	
Truck	$45,000.00
Accumulated amortization of truck	-$750.00
Computer	$5,600.00
Accumulated amortization of computer	-$101.39
	$49,748.61
Total Assets	$561,035.72
LIABILITIES	
Current liabilities	
Account payable	$37,000.00
Interest payable	$3,000.00
	$40,000.00
Long term liabilities	
Note payable	$500,000.00
Total Liability	$540,000.00

SHAREHOLDERS' EQUITY	
Owners' capital	
Share capital	$10,000.00
Retined earnings	$0.00
Accumulated other comprehensive income	$0.00
Total Shareholders' Equity	$10,000.00
Total Liabilities and Shareholders' Equity	$550,000.00

Figure 3-5   Balance Sheet without Including Net Income

Clicking the CashFlows box gets the cash flows statement. It tells me how the cash amounts changes during a period. From this idea, I can get a new concept: account flows statement if an account has the two-level subaccounts.

Clicking the AccountFlows box and entering the inventory account, I get the Figure 3-6 which shows the inventory flows. Because the inventory has four one-level subaccounts, the inventory flows statement only shows the top three balances of the one-level subaccounts. The ending inventory for the top three one-level subaccounts is $17,370 while total ending inventory is $18,870. The difference between them is $1,500 which is the balance of the one-level subaccount Inven1.

MathAccounting	
Inventory Flows Statement	
Inventory Flows Statement Year Ended 2014-01-31	
Inven4	
Inven41	$8,800.00
RRRHJK parts	$1,400.00
TTT parts	$2,300.00
Net Inventory provided by Inven4	$12,500.00
Inven3	
ASDUP parts	$500.00
Inven31	$400.00
Inven32	$1,100.00
Inven33	$700.00
QASXC parts	$100.00
Net Inventory provided by Inven3	$2,800.00
Inven2	
ASD parts	$1,200.00
Inven21	$270.00
Inven22	$600.00
Net Inventory provided by Inven2	$2,070.00
Net change in Inventory	$17,370.00
Inventory, Begining	$0.00
Inventory, Ending	$17,370.00
Total Inventory, Ending	$18,870.00

Figure 3-6   Inventory Flows Statement

The followings are the transactions for the second month:

- On February 1, 2014, RR Company purchases the supplies for cash $103.3.
- On February 3, 2014, RR Company purchases $91,000 inventory on credit from D1 Company (phone number: 987654323).

  The inventory's multi-subaccounts are:

  "HGFCVB parts<QASXC parts<Inven3" for $10*5960,

  "PPGHUP parts<ASDUP parts<Inven3" for $10*3140.

- On February 4, 2014, Jun Wang sales $91,200 inventory to E1 Company (phone number: 123456788) on credit $177,600.

  The inventory's multi-subaccounts are:

  "HGFCVB parts<QASXC parts<Inven3" of cost -$10*5960,

  "PPGHUP parts<ASDUP parts<Inven3" of cost -$10*3160.

- On February 8, 2014, RR Company receives $5,000 cash from B1 Company (phone number: 123456789) with the General ID 25.

- On February 9, 2014, RR Company receives $10,000 cash from F1Company (phone number: 123456787) with the General ID 14 ($6700) and the General ID 22 ($3300).

- On February 11, 2014, RR Company receives $3,500 cash from H1Company (phone number: 123456786) with the General ID 23.

- On February 13, 2014, RR Company pays $2,500 cash to A1Company (phone number: 987654321) with the General ID 4.

- On February 15, 2014, RR Company pays $15,000 cash to C1Company (phone number: 987654322) with the General ID 21.

- On February 17, 2014, RR Company spays $4,000 cash to D1Company (phone number: 987654323) with the General ID 11.

- On February 18, 2014, RR Company sells land1 (downtown) for $360,000 cash.

  The transaction sub-equation is:

  Cash (1): 360000 + Land (1): -270000 = Investment income (4): 90000

  For the parent account "Investment income, the "Subtotal name" should be the "Other income, 475", so the parent account "Investment Income" row number is the "476".

- On the same day, RR Company purchases 10,000 the MicroQQ Company shares for $35.67 each share. Total amount is $356,700.

- On February 25, 2014, RR Company receives $120,000 cash from E1 Company (phone number: 123456788) with the General ID 48.

- On February 26, 2014, RR Company pays $55,000 cash to D1Company (phone number: 987654323) with the General ID 47.

- On February 28, 2014, RR Company pays $55.32 cash to Dan Zhu (Purchase department) for the other expenses.

- On the same day, RR Company pays $458.39 cash to Hua Li (Purchase department) for the travelling expenses $336.41 and the other expenses $121.98.

- On the same day, RR Company pays $33.72 cash to Xiao Zhou (Sales department) for the other expenses.

- On the same day, RR Company pays $152.31 cash to Jun Wang (Sales department) for the travelling expenses.

- On the same day, RR Company pays $1,015.98 cash to Zhendao Yuan (Sales department) for the other expenses.

- On the same day, RR Company pays $117.95 cash to Yi Liu (Sales department) for the travelling expenses $99.8 and the other expenses $18.15.

- On the same day, RR Company records the office supplies expenses $101.28.

- On the same day, RR Company pays $18,756 cash for all salary of February, 2014.

- On the same day, RR Company records the truck's amortization expenses $750 one month (5 years, straight line, and second month).

- On the same day, RR Company records the second month computers' amortization expenses ($202.78).

The computer account has three one-level subaccounts of the computer1 ($66.67), the computer server ($75), and the POS system ($61.11). The transaction sub-equation is:

Accumulated amortization: computer (1) -66.67 + Accumulated amortization: computer (1) -75 + Accumulated amortization: computer (1) -61.11 = - Amortization expenses (5) 66.67 - Amortization expenses (5) 75 - amortization expenses (5) 61.11

The left three items of the equation belong to the same account. It has three one-level subaccounts which are the "Computer1-accumulated amortization", the "Computer server-accumulated amortization", and the "POS system-accumulated amortization". The right three items of the equation have respectively their two-level subaccounts which are the "Computer1-amortization<Computer- amortization", the "Computer server-amortization<Computer-amortization", and the "POS system - amortization Computer- amortization". The Figure 3-7 shows the detail information of the subaccount "POS system- accumulated amortization".

MathAccounting

Accumulated amortization:Computer: POS system-accumulated amo

ID	Multi-Name	Amount	Unit	General ID	Transaction Date
3	POS system-accumulated amortization	-$30.56	1	39	2014-01-31
6	POS system-accumulated amortization	-$61.11	1	67	2014-02-28
		-$91.67	2		

Figure 3-7   Subaccount of the POS System-accumulated Amortization

- On the same day, RR Company pays $293.37 cash for the utility expenses.
- On the same day, RR Company pays $1,500 cash for the office rent expenses.
- On the same day, RR Company records the note payable's interest expenses $3,333.33 and the accrued interest payable (500,000*8%/12).

If RR Company ends its first fiscal year on February 28, 2014, I can get the Figure 3-8 (seeing the next page) by clicking the IncomeStatement box. The Figure 3-8 shows the earnings before income taxes: $160,665.29. If the income tax rate is 0.3, then the tax payable is: $160,665.29*0.3 = 48,199.59 and the net earnings is: $160,665.29 - $48,199.59 = $112,465.70.

Earnings Before tax = 160665.2900 and Net Earnings = 112465.70300

OK

Income Statement

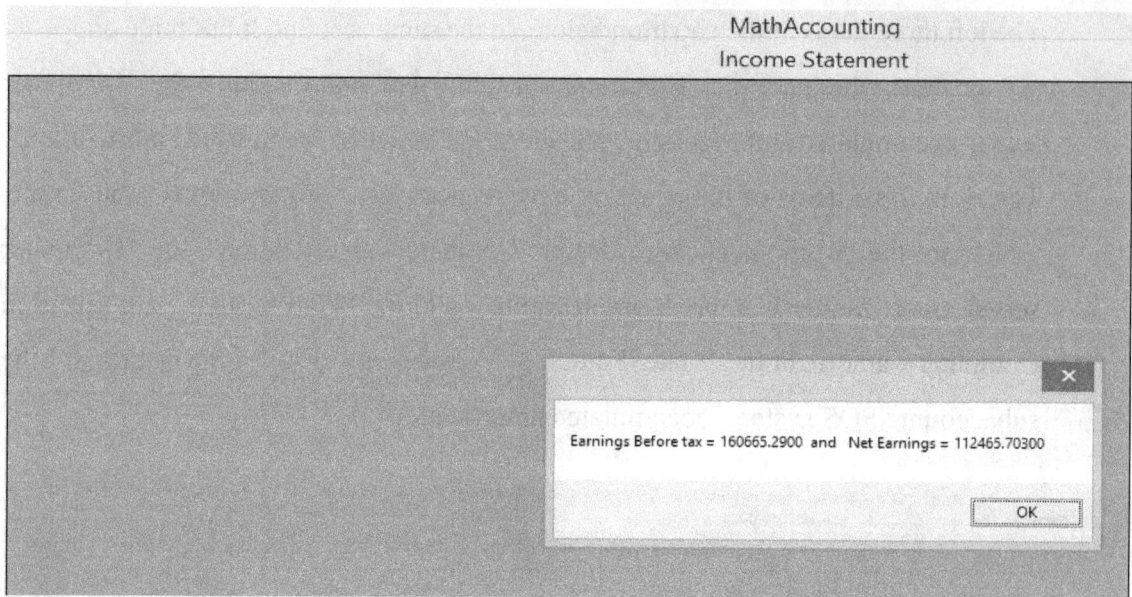

Year ended: 2/28/2014	
Revenues	
Sales	$271,130.00
Cost	
Cost of sales	-$147,000.00
Gross Margin	$124,130.00
Operating and administrative expenses	
Travelling expenses	-$1,838.03
Other expenses	-$2,213.83
Supplies expenses	-$189.28
Salary expenses	-$37,512.00
Amortization expenses	-$1,804.17
Utility expenses	-$574.07
Rent expenses	-$3,000.00
Interest expenses	-$6,333.33
Other revenue	
Investing income	$90,000.00
Earnings Before Income Taxes	$160,665.29
Net Earnings	$160,665.29
Retained Earnings,Begining	$0.00
Retained Earnings,Ending	$160,665.29

Figure 3-8   Getting Earnings before Income Tax

To get the income statement, balance sheet, cash flows, and comprehensive income statement and begin a new fiscal year, I need enter the following transactions.

- On February 28, 2014, RR Company records the tax expenses $48,199.59 and the tax payable $48,199.59.

  After entering the transaction, the net earnings will transfer into the end retained earnings.

- On the same day, RR Company records the land's unrealized holding gain or loss. The land (land2, North York) has fair price of $210,000.

  Due to the land being the AFS investment, I must calculate the unrealized holding gain or loss (OCI) and the accumulated other comprehensive income (AOCI). A similar method of dealing with the accumulated amortization account can be used for dealing with the accumulated other comprehensive income (AOCI) account. So the accumulated other comprehensive income (AOCI) account is also a contra account of the land account.

  The Unrealized holding gain or loss account, which is the difference between the fair price and the cost price, will be put into the fourth class accounts. If the amount of this account is negative, it means the unrealized holding loss. The fair price is $210,000 and the cost is $180,000, so the sub-equation is:

  Accumulated other comprehensive income of land (1): 30000 = Unrealized holding gain or loss (4): 30000

Here, you must pay attention that the increase of the "Accumulated other comprehensive income (AOCI)" means the "+" because I put the "Unrealized holding gain or loss" into the fourth class accounts.

  If you wish put the "Unrealized holding gain or loss" into the fifth class accounts, then the meaning of the "Accumulated other comprehensive income (AOCI)" account's increasing or decreasing is as same as the "Accumulated amortization" account's.

  The "Accumulated other comprehensive income: land" account and the

"Unrealized holding gain or loss" account all have the one-level subaccounts, and their Subtotal names are the "Long term investments, 141" and the "Other comprehensive income, 713" respectively.

- On the same day, RR Company records the share's unrealized holding gain or loss. The share's market price is $35.21 each share.

    The transaction is the same as the previous transaction. The unrealized holding gain or loss of the MicroQQ share is -$4,600. The transaction sub-equation is:

    Accumulated other comprehensive income: share (1): -4600 = Unrealized holding gain or loss (4): -4600

The Figure 3-9, Figure 3-10 (after beginning new fiscal year), Figure 3-11, and Figure 3-12 respectively show the RR Company's four tables: Income statement, Balance sheet, Cash flows, and Comprehensive income statement, seeing the following pages.

Income Statement	
Year ended: 2/28/2014	
Revenues	
Sales	$271,130.00
Cost	
Cost of sales	-$147,000.00
Gross Margin	$124,130.00
Operating and administrative expenses,453	
Travelling expenses	-$1,838.03
Other expenses	-$2,213.83
Office supplies expenses	-$189.28
Salary expenses	-$37,512.00
Amortization expenses	-$1,804.17
Utility expenses	-$574.07
Office rent expenses	-$3,000.00
Interest expenses	-$6,333.33
Other income	
Investment income	$90,000.00
Earnings Before Income Taxes	$160,665.29
Tax	
Tax expenses	-$48,199.59
Net Earnings	$112,465.70
Retained Earnings,Begining	$0.00
Retained Earnings,Ending	$112,465.70

Figure 3-9   Income Statement

Balance Sheet

As at 2/28/2014	
ASSETS	
Current assets	
Cash	$54,395.77
Supplies	$107.02
Inventory	$18,670.00
Account receivable	$69,830.00
	$143,002.79
Long term investments	
Land	$180,000.00
AOCI: land	$30,000.00
Share	$356,700.00
AOCI: share	-$4,600.00
	$562,100.00
Equipments	
Truck	$45,000.00
Accumulated amortization:Truck	-$1,500.00
Computer	$5,600.00
Accumulated amortization:Computer	-$304.17
	$48,795.83
Total Assets	$753,898.62
LIABILITIES	
Current liabilities	
Account payable	$51,500.00
Accrued interest payable	$6,333.33
Tax payable	$48,199.59
	$106,032.92
Long term liabilities	
Note payable	$500,000.00
Total Liability	$606,032.92
SHAREHOLDERS' EQUITY	
Owners' capital	
Share capital	$10,000.00
Retined earnings	$112,465.70
Accumulated other comprehensive income	$25,400.00
Total Shareholders' Equity	$147,865.70
Total Liabilities and Shareholders' Equity	$753,898.62

Figure 3-10   Balance Sheet

RR Company has gotten the long term investment for sale. The Figure 3-10 shows the cost of the investments and their accumulated other comprehensive incomes which are respectively under the subtotal name of the "Long term investment". The total accumulated other comprehensive income is under the subtotal name of the "Owners' capital".

The Figure 3-11 on the next page shows that the amounts of the "Cash" account at the beginning of a fiscal year and at the ending of a fiscal are $0 and $54,395.77 respectively. Its change during the fiscal year is $54,395.77(=$54,395.77-$0).

Cash Flow Statement	
Cash Flows Statement Year Ended 2014-02-28	
Operating activities	
Cash payment for operating expenses	-$45,434.23
Cash payment to suppliers	-$164,770.00
Cash receipts from customers	$201,300.00
Net cash provided by Operating activities	-$8,904.23
Investing activities	
Cash payments for investment	-$806,700.00
Cash receipts from other customers	$360,000.00
Net cash provided by Investing activities	-$446,700.00
Financing activities	
Cash receipts from banks	$500,000.00
Cash receipts from owners	$10,000.00
Net cash provided by Financing activities	$510,000.00
Net change in cash	$54,395.77
Cash, Begining	$0.00
Cash, Ending	$54,395.77

Figure 3-11   Cash Flows Statement

Comprehensive Income Statement	
Year ended: 2/28/2014	
Net Income	$112,465.70
Other Comprehensive Income	
Unrealized holding gain or loss, net of tax	$25,400.00
Comprehensive Income	$137,865.70

Figure 3-12   Comprehensive Income Statements

The Figure 3-12 shows the total unrealized holding gain or loss $25,400 which is consisted of the land's unrealized holding gain or loss $30,000 and the MicroQQ share's unrealized holding gain or loss -$4,600.

For beginning a new fiscal year, I click the IncomeStatement box and answer the "Yes" for the question of the "Would you like to begin new fiscal year?" in the Figure 3-13. Of course, I must do the YearBackup before doing this.

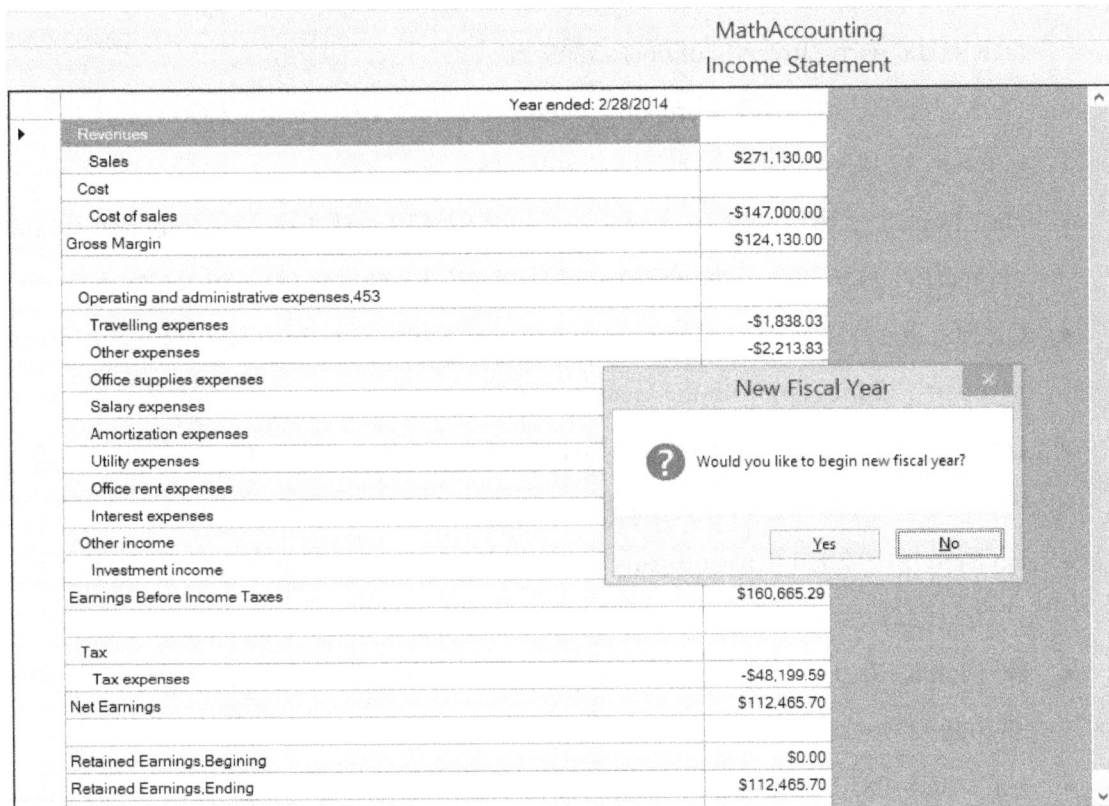

MathAccounting
Income Statement

Year ended: 2/28/2014	
Revenues	
Sales	$271,130.00
Cost	
Cost of sales	-$147,000.00
Gross Margin	$124,130.00
Operating and administrative expenses,453	
Travelling expenses	-$1,838.03
Other expenses	-$2,213.83
Office supplies expenses	
Salary expenses	
Amortization expenses	
Utility expenses	
Office rent expenses	
Interest expenses	
Other income	
Investment income	
Earnings Before Income Taxes	$160,665.29
Tax	
Tax expenses	-$48,199.59
Net Earnings	$112,465.70
Retained Earnings.Begining	$0.00
Retained Earnings.Ending	$112,465.70

New Fiscal Year

Would you like to begin new fiscal year?

Yes   No

Figure 3-13   Income Statement interface

3.2 Begin second fiscal year

In the new fiscal year, I will enter the following transactions.

- On March 2, 2014, RR Company purchases the supplies for cash $123.87.
- On March 3, 2014, RR Company purchases the $85,360 inventory on credit from G1 Company (phone number: 987654324).

The inventory's multi-subaccounts are:

"TTTCU parts<TTT parts<Inven4" for $2*33105,

"RRRHJK parts<Inven4" for $ 2*9575.

- On March 4, 2014, Yi Liu sales $85,200 inventory to F1 Company (phone number: 123456787) on credit $154,800.

  The inventory's multi-subaccounts are:

  "TTTCU parts<TTT parts<Inven4" of cost -$2*33035,

  "RRRHJK parts<Inven4" of cost -$2*9565.

- On March 10, 2014, RR Company receives $52,000 cash from E1 Company (phone number: 123456788) with the General ID 48.

- On March 12, 2014, RR Company receives $1,430 cash from B1Company (phone number: 123456789) with the General ID 5 ($230) and the General ID 25 ($1200).

- On March 13, 2014, RR Company receives $2,200 cash from H1Company (phone number: 123456786) with the General ID 23.

- On March 14, 2014, RR Company pays $500 cash to A1Company (phone number: 987654321) with the General ID 4.

- On March 15, 2014, RR Company pays $4,500 cash to C1Company (phone number: 987654322) with the General ID 21.

- On March 17, 2014, RR Company pays $30,000 cash to D1Company (phone number: 987654323) with the General ID 47.

- On March 28, 2014, RR Company pays $153.72 cash to Mike Newsome (Office department) for the other expenses.

- On March 29, 2014, RR Company receives $120,000 cash from F1Company (phone number: 123456787) with the General ID 78.

- On same day, RR Company pays $82,360 cash to G1Company (phone number: 987654324) with the General ID 77.

- On the same day, RR Company pays $171.63 cash to Hua Li (Purchase department) for travelling expenses $101.33 and the other expenses $70.30.

- On the same day, RR Company pays $52.17 cash to Xiao Zhou (Sales department) the other expenses.

- On the same day, RR Company pays $129.34 cash to Jun Wang (Sales department) for the travelling expenses.

- On the same day, RR Company pays $111.93 cash to Zhendao Yuan (Sales department) for the other expenses.

- On March 30, 2014, RR Company pays $1,210.91 cash to Yi Liu (Sales department) for the travelling expenses $1132.56 and the other expenses $78.35.

- On the same day, RR Company pays $201.99 cash to Ping Wang (Office department) for the other expenses.

- On March 31, 2014, RR Company records the office supplies expenses $101.28.

- On the same day, RR Company pays $23,790 cash for all salary of March, 2014.

- On the same day, RR Company records the truck's amortization expenses $750 one month (5 years, straight line, and third month).

- On the same day, RR Company records the computers' amortization expenses ($202.78).

    The computer account has three one-level subaccounts of the computer1 ($66.67), the computer server ($75), and the POS system ($61.11).

- On the same day, RR Company pays $323.14 cash for the utility expenses.

- On the same day, RR Company pays $1,500 cash for the office rent expenses.

- On the same day, RR Company records the note payable's interest expenses $3,333.33 and the accrued interest payable (500,000*8%/12).

The Figure 3-14 (seeing the next page) shows the income statement without entering the tax expenses and beginning a new fiscal year. From the Figure 3-14, the earnings before income taxes is equal to the net earnings $37,567.78. The difference between the total assets ($762,799.73) and the total liabilities and shareholders' equity ($725,231.95) in the Figure 3-15 (following the Figure 3-14) is just equal to the earnings before income taxes $37,567.78.

Income Statement	
Year ended: 3/31/2014	
Revenues	
Sales	$154,800.00
Cost	
Cost of sales	-$85,200.00
Gross Margin	$69,600.00
Operating and administrative expenses,453	
Travelling expenses	-$1,363.23
Other expenses	-$668.46
Office supplies expenses	-$101.28
Salary expenses	-$23,790.00
Amortization expenses	-$952.78
Utility expenses	-$323.14
Office rent expenses	-$1,500.00
Interest expenses	-$3,333.33
Other income	
Investment income	$0.00
Earnings Before Income Taxes	$37,567.78
Tax	
Tax expenses	$0.00
Net Earnings	$37,567.78
Retained Earnings,Begining	$112,465.70
Retained Earnings,Ending	$150,033.48

Figure 3-14   Income Statements without Entering Tax Expenses

As at 3/31/2014	
ASSETS	
Current assets	
Cash	$84,897.07
Supplies	$129.61
Inventory	$18,830.00
Account receivable	$49,000.00
	$152,856.68
Long term investments	
Land	$180,000.00
AOCI: land	$55,000.00
Share	$356,700.00
AOCI: share	$41,100.00
	$632,800.00
Equipments	
Truck	$45,000.00
Accumulated amortization:Truck	-$2,250.00
Computer	$5,600.00
Accumulated amortization:Computer	-$506.95
	$47,843.05
Total Assets	$833,499.73
LIABILITIES	
Current liabilities	
Account payable	$19,500.00
Accrued interest payable	$9,666.66
Note payable	$500,000.00
Total Liability	$577,366.25
SHAREHOLDERS' EQUITY	
Owners' capital	
Share capital	$10,000.00
Retined earnings	$112,465.70
Accumulated other comprehensive income	$25,400.00
Total Shareholders' Equity	$147,865.70
Total Liabilities and Shareholders' Equity	$725,231.95

Figure 3-15   Balance Sheets without Beginning New Fiscal Year

If I will begin a new fiscal year on April 1, 2014 to check whether the income statement and the balance sheet are correct, I must enter following transactions.

- On March 31, 2014, RR Company records the tax expenses $11,270.33 and tax payable $11,270.33, and the net earnings will transfer into the ending retained earnings.

- On the same day, RR Company records the land's unrealized holding gain or loss. The land (land2, North York) has fair price of $235,000.

  The Unrealized holding gain or loss account is now the difference between the fair price and the carrying value. The fair price is $235,000 and the carrying value is $210,000, so the transaction sub-equation is:

Accumulated other comprehensive income: land (1): 25000 = Unrealized holding gain or loss (4): 25000

The "Accumulated other comprehensive income: Land" and the "Unrealized holding gain or loss" accounts all have the one-level subaccounts.

- On the same day, RR Company records the share's market price is $39.78 each share. The transaction is the same as the previous transaction. The unrealized holding gain or loss of MicroQQ is $45,700, and the transaction sub-equation is:

Accumulated other comprehensive income: share (1): 45700 = Unrealized holding gain or loss (4): 45700

After answering the "Yes" for the question "Would you like to begin new fiscal year?", I get the income statement, balance sheet, cash flows (including the cash account table), and comprehensive income statement in the Figure 3-16 to the Figure 3-19 (seeing the following pages). Please notice the changes of the AOCI, the Accumulated amortization, the Cash (Beginning) and the Cash (Ending).

Year ended: 2/28/2015	
Revenues	
Sales	$154,800.00
Cost	
Cost of sales	-$85,200.00
Gross Margin	$69,600.00
Operating and administrative expenses,453	
Travelling expenses	-$1,363.23
Other expenses	-$668.46
Office supplies expenses	-$101.28
Salary expenses	-$23,790.00
Amortization expenses	-$952.78
Utility expenses	-$323.14
Office rent expenses	-$1,500.00
Interest expenses	-$3,333.33
Other income	
Investment income	$0.00
Earnings Before Income Taxes	$37,567.78
Tax	
Tax expenses	-$11,270.33
Net Earnings	$26,297.45
Retained Earnings,Begining	$112,465.70
Retained Earnings,Ending	$138,763.15

Figure 3-16   Income Statement

Balance Sheet

As at 2/28/2015	
ASSETS	
Current assets	
Cash	$84,897.07
Supplies	$129.61
Inventory	$18,830.00
Account receivable	$49,000.00
	$152,856.68
Long term investments	
Land	$180,000.00
AOCI: land	$55,000.00
Share	$356,700.00
AOCI: share	$41,100.00
	$632,800.00
Equipments	
Truck	$45,000.00
Accumulated amortization:Truck	-$2,250.00
Computer	$5,600.00
Accumulated amortization:Computer	-$506.95
	$47,843.05
Total Assets	$833,499.73
LIABILITIES	
Current liabilities	
Account payable	$19,500.00
Accrued interest payable	$9,666.66
Tax payable	$59,469.92
	$88,636.58
Long term liabilities	
Note payable	$500,000.00
Total Liability	$588,636.58
SHAREHOLDERS' EQUITY	
Owners' capital	
Share capital	$10,000.00
Retined earnings	$138,763.15
Accumulated other comprehensive income	$96,100.00
Total Shareholders' Equity	$244,863.15
Total Liabilities and Shareholders' Equity	$833,499.73

Figure 3-17   Balance Sheets with Beginning New Fiscal Year

Cash Flow Statement

Cash Flows Statement Year Ended 2015-02-28	
Operating activities	
Cash payment for operating expenses	-$27,768.70
Cash payment to suppliers	-$117,360.00
Cash receipts from customers	$175,630.00
Net cash provided by Operating activities	$30,501.30
Investing activities	
Net cash provided by Investing activities	$0.00
Financing activities	
Net cash provided by Financing activities	$0.00
Net change in cash	$30,501.30
Cash, Begining	$54,395.77
Cash, Ending	$84,897.07

Cash

ID	Multi-Name	Amount	Balance	General ID	Transaction Date	Reference(Row)
51	Cash payment for operating expenses<Op...	-$18,756.00	$56,087.86	65	2014-02-28	
52	Cash payment for operating expenses<Op...	-$293.37	$55,794.49	68	2014-02-28	
53	Cash payment for operating expenses<Op...	-$1,500.00	$54,294.49	69	2014-02-28	
54	Cash payment for operating expenses<Op...	$101.28	$54,395.77	74	2014-02-28	
55	Cash receipts from customers<Operating a...	$52,000.00	$106,395.77	77	2014-03-10	
56	Cash receipts from customers<Operating a...	$1,430.00	$107,825.77	78	2014-03-12	
57	Cash receipts from customers<Operating a...	$2,200.00	$110,025.77	79	2014-03-13	
58	Cash payment to suppliers<Operating activ...	-$500.00	$109,525.77	80	2014-03-14	
59	Cash payment to suppliers<Operating activ...	-$4,500.00	$105,025.77	81	2014-03-15	
60	Cash payment to suppliers<Operating activ...	-$30,000.00	$75,025.77	82	2014-03-17	
61	Cash payment for operating expenses<Op...	-$153.72	$74,872.05	83	2014-03-28	
62	Cash receipts from customers<Operating a...	$120,000.00	$194,872.05	84	2014-03-29	
63	Cash payment to suppliers<Operating activ...	-$82,360.00	$112,512.05	85	2014-03-29	
64	Cash payment for operating expenses<Op...	-$171.63	$112,340.42	86	2014-03-29	
65	Cash payment for operating expenses<Op...	-$52.17	$112,288.25	87	2014-03-29	
66	Cash payment for operating expenses<Op...	-$129.34	$112,158.91	88	2014-03-29	
67	Cash payment for operating expenses<Op...	-$111.93	$112,046.98	89	2014-03-29	
68	Cash payment for operating expenses<Op...	-$1,210.91	$110,836.07	90	2014-03-30	
69	Cash payment for operating expenses<Op...	-$201.99	$110,634.08	91	2014-03-30	
70	Cash payment for operating expenses<Op...	-$23,790.00	$86,844.08	93	2014-03-31	
71	Cash payment for operating expenses<Op...	-$323.14	$86,520.94	96	2014-03-31	
72	Cash payment for operating expenses<Op...	-$1,500.00	$85,020.94	97	2014-03-31	
73	Cash payment for operating expenses<Op...	-$123.87	$84,897.07	102	2014-03-02	

Figure 3-18   Cash Flows Statement and Cash Account

	MathAccounting	
	Comprehensive Income Statement	
Year ended: 2/28/2015		
▶ Net Income		$26,297.45
Other Comprehensive Income		
Unrealized holding gain or loss, net of tax		$70,700.00
Comprehensive Income		$96,997.45
∗		

Figure 3-19   Comprehensive Income Statements

3.3 Convert to MathAccounting software during fiscal year

If a company will like to use the MathAccounting software during its current fiscal year, it is easy to begin the mathematical accounting model. For any company, the balances of all accounts are satisfied the dynamic accounting equation, so you can enter a transaction which includes all the accounts and their related information to complete the transference in theory. However, because of the limtion of maximum eight entries in a transaction (I will increase the entries' number in a transaction later), you must divide the dynamic accounting equation into the N sub-equations. No matter how you combine the accounts in a transaction, the only requirement is that each sub-equation must be balanced exception of the "Account receivable" and the "Account payable" accounts.

Because the MathAccounting software needs the transaction dates of the "Account receivable" and the "Account payable" accounts, only the same transaction date of account receivable and account payable can be combined into a new transaction in the MathAccounting software. The following is a example.

For a customer (phone number: 567891234), the detail information of its account receivable account is:

Trancaction date: Janurary 3, 2014, amount: $980,

Trancaction date: Janurary 19, 2014, amount: $1,230,

Trancaction date: Feruary 27, 2014, amount: $5,500.

For a supplier (phone number: 123498765), the detail information of its account payable account is:

Trancaction date: Janurary 8, 2014, amount: $1,400,

Trancaction date: Janurary 19, 2014, amount: $1,860,

Trancaction date: Feruary 28, 2014, amount: $6,900.

Then, the account receivable and account payable with same transaction date can be combined into a new transaction in the MathAccounting software. The new transaction equation may be:

Account receivable (1): 1230 + Cash (1): 630 = Account payable (2): 1860

Here, cash $630 is only the part of the cash account's balance. Of course, you can add more items to the sub-equation until the maximum number of eight items to make the sub-equation be equal.

Chapter 4

Introduction of SQL Server

Now, I will simply introduce SQL Server and look at how the SQL Server works and what the SQL Server do for us behind the screen. Of course, Oracle database cab also be used in the MathAccounting software.

SQL Server 2012 is a powerful database and its security is guaranteed by three levels of principles: Windows, SQL server, and Database.

The "behind the screen" means that you can use the MathAccounting software even without understanding the SQL Server. After executing the SQL Server and entering password, I click the small box with the "+" beside the databases at the left of the screen, and then click the small box with the "+" beside the jgp1 again, and get the first figure in the Figure 4-1. For database jgp1, I am interested in the tables, so I click the small box beside the tables and get all tables, seeing the other figures in the Figure 4-1.

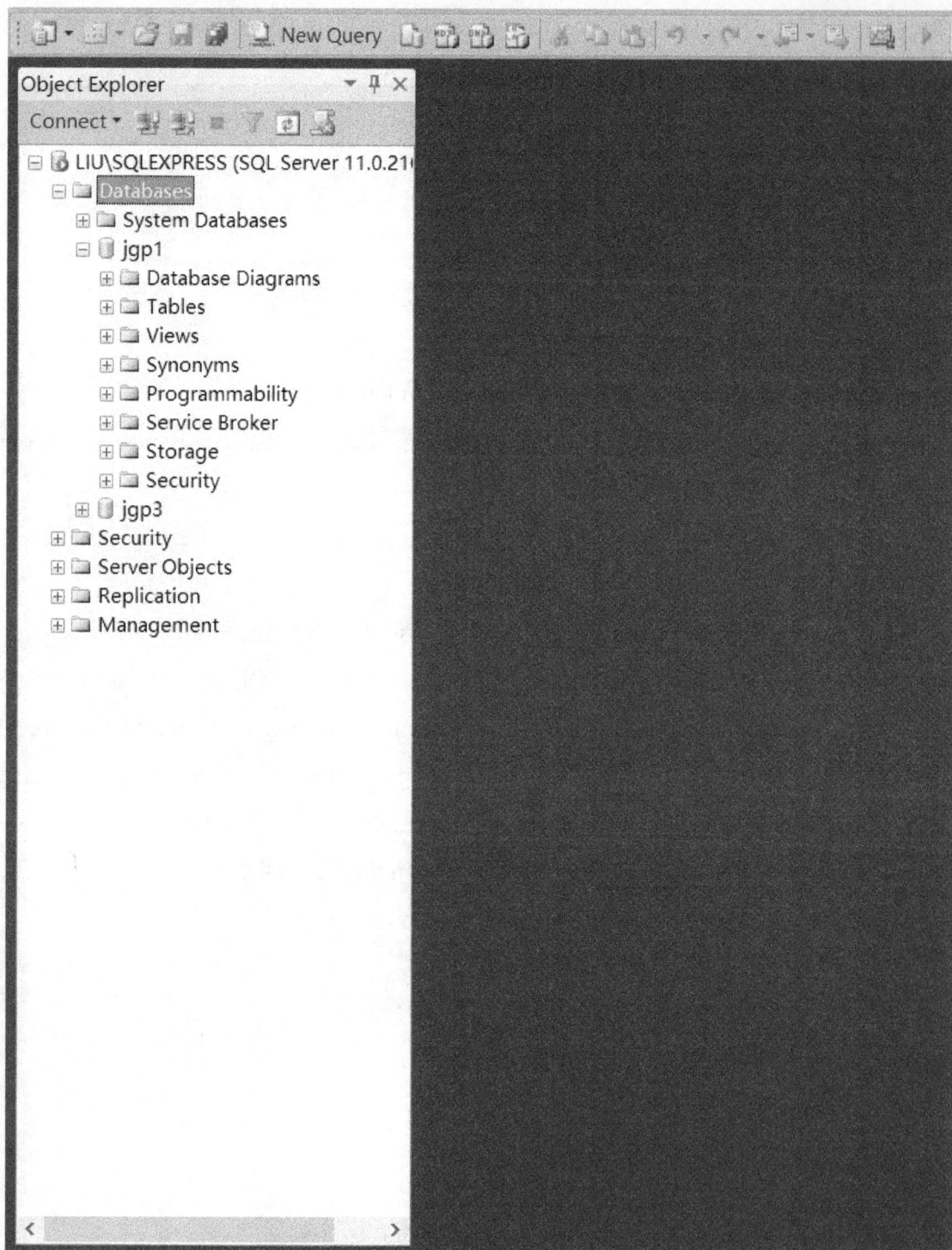

Figure 4-1   Database jgp1 and All Tables (Continue)

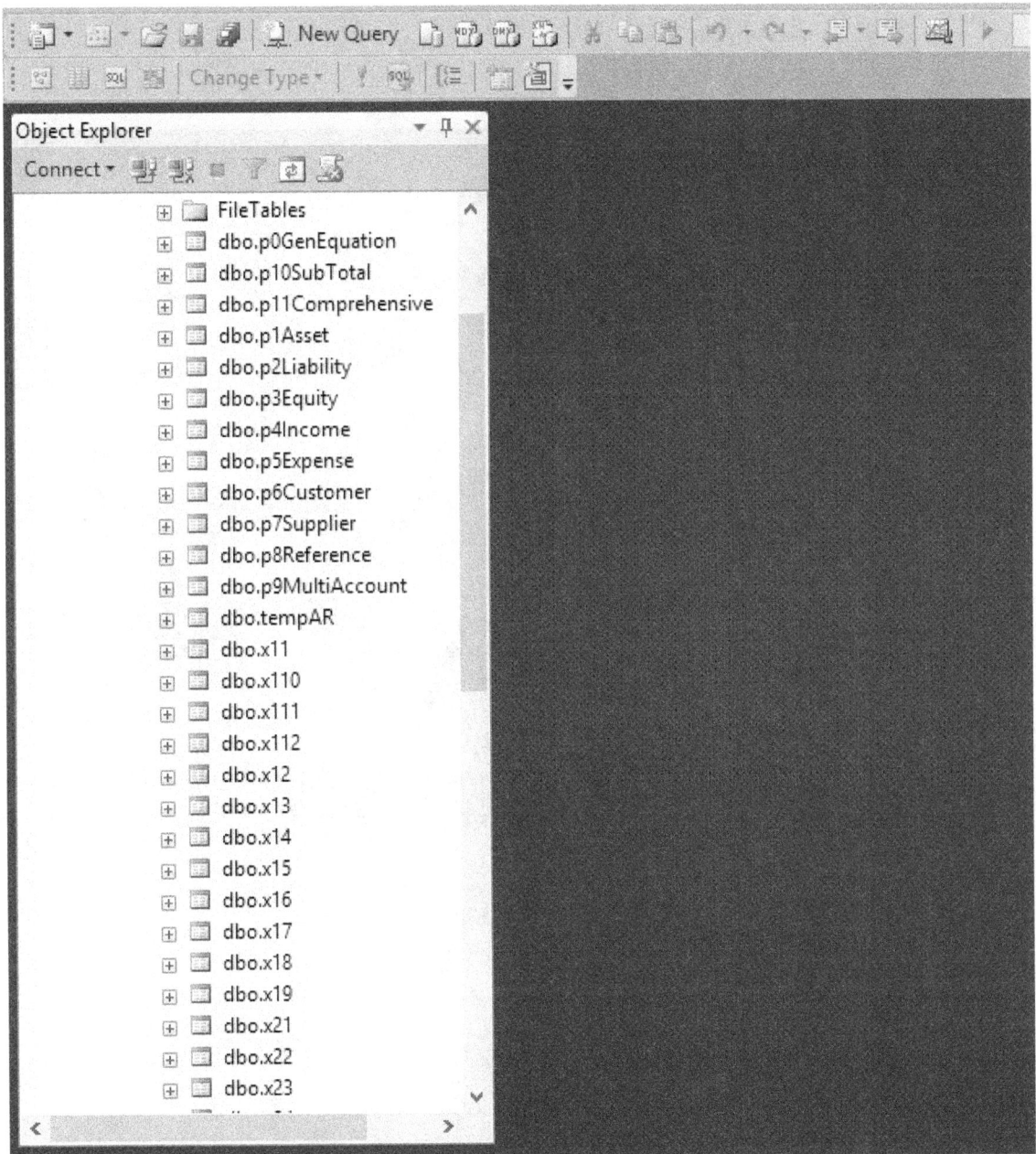

Figure 4-1   Database jgp1 and All Tables (Continue)

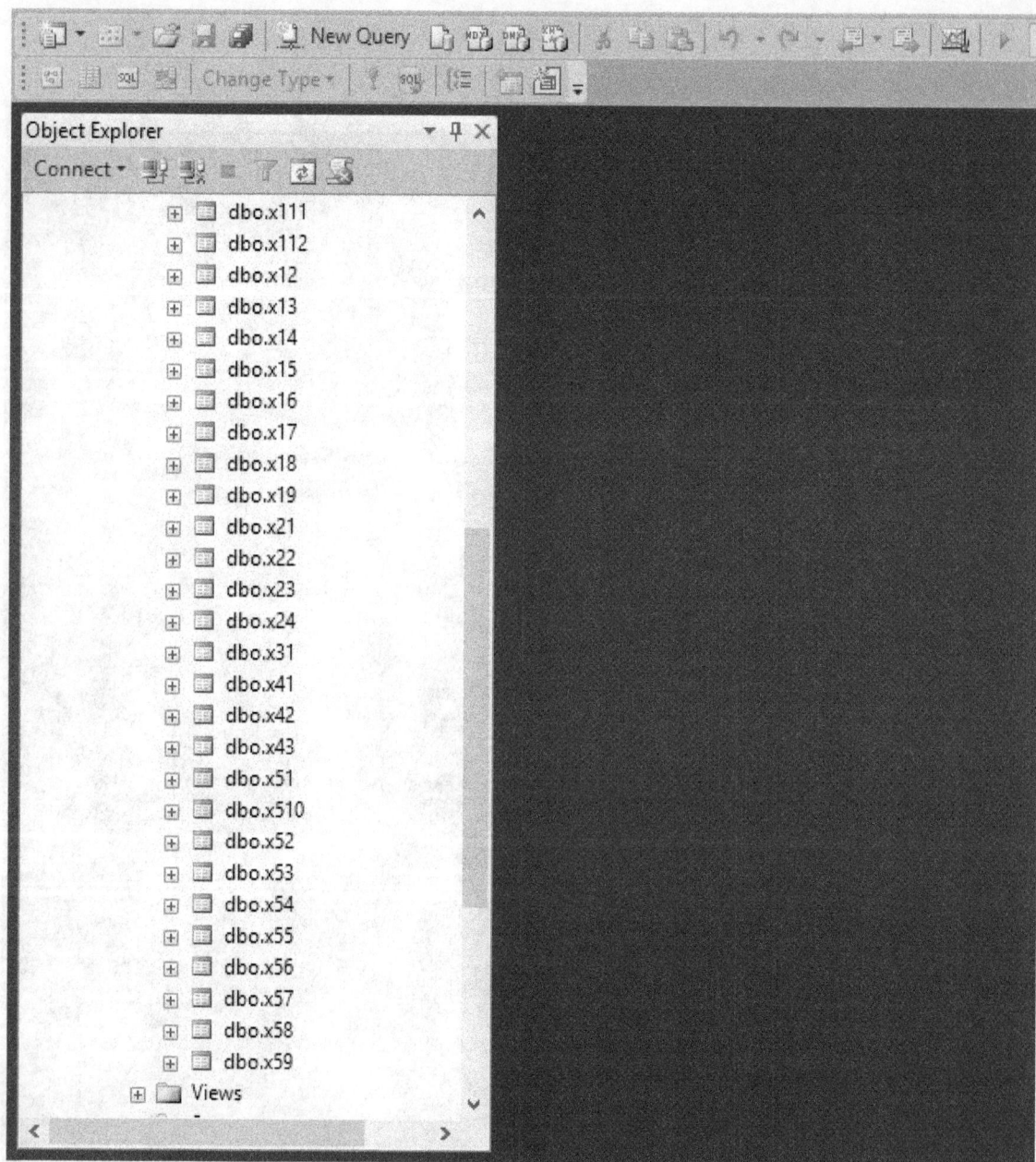

Figure 4-1   Database jgp1 and All Tables

The SQL Server has built many tables for the company. You should understand what the top twelve tables mean from their names. The first Table should be the General equation table. However, what are the tables of x11, x12, and x21…? In fact, I use a similar method as the coordinate exchange in the numerical calculation in programming the MathAccounting software. By using of this method, I exchange the real names of all parent accounts, which I enter into the database in the transaction function model, to the mathematical names according to their entering order number. Then the computer can categorize and calculate them. I use the "New Query" to show two tables of the p0GenEquation and the x13 in the Figure 4-2 (seeing this page and the next page). The table p0GenEquation is indeed the "General equation" table and the x13 table is the "Inventory" table. Because the "Inventory" account is thirdly entered into 1 class accounts, the name of the "Inventory" account has exchanged to the mathematical name of the "x13".

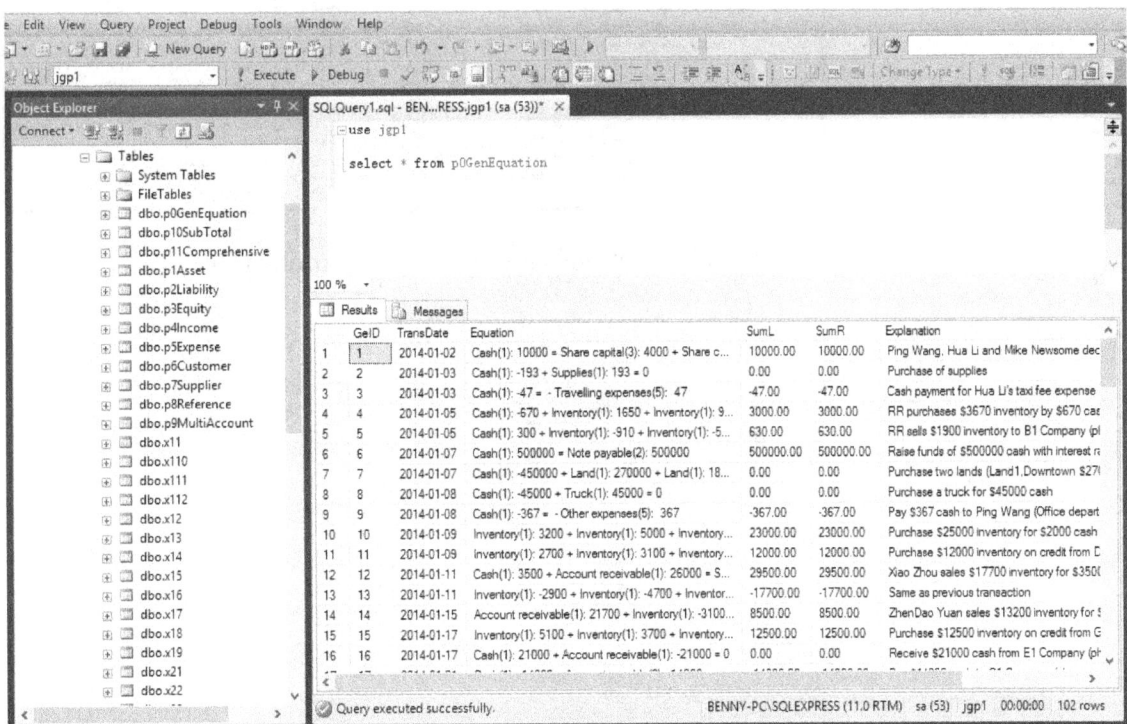

Figure 4-2   General Equations and Inventory Account Table (Continue)

Figure 4-2 General Equations and Inventory Account Table

The screen shows an SQL Server Management Studio window. The query pane contains:

```
use jgp1

select * from x13
```

The Object Explorer tree (Tables) lists:
- System Tables
- FileTables
- dbo.p0GenEquation
- dbo.p10SubTotal
- dbo.p11Comprehensive
- dbo.p1Asset
- dbo.p2Liability
- dbo.p3Equity
- dbo.p4Income
- dbo.p5Expense
- dbo.p6Customer
- dbo.p7Supplier
- dbo.p8Reference
- dbo.p9MultiAccount
- dbo.x11
- dbo.x110
- dbo.x111
- dbo.x112
- dbo.x12
- dbo.x13
- dbo.x14
- dbo.x15
- dbo.x16
- dbo.x17
- dbo.x18
- dbo.x19
- dbo.x21
- dbo.x22

Results grid:

	IDall	multiName	Amount	Reference	Balance	GeID	subFirst	subSecond	subThird	Unit
1	1	Inven111<Inven11<Inven1	1650.00		1650.00	4	Inven1	Inven11	Inven111	165
2	2	Inven112<Inven11<Inven1	900.00		2550.00	4	Inven1	Inven11	Inven112	225
3	3	Inven121<Inven12<Inven1	520.00		3070.00	4	Inven1	Inven12	Inven121	650
4	4	Inven122<Inven12<Inven1	330.00		3400.00	4	Inven1	Inven12	Inven122	66
5	5	Inven21<Inven2	270.00		3670.00	4	Inven2	Inven21		9
6	6	Inven111<Inven11<Inven1	-910.00		2760.00	5	Inven1	Inven11	Inven111	-91
7	7	Inven112<Inven11<Inven1	-520.00		2240.00	5	Inven1	Inven11	Inven112	-130
8	8	Inven121<Inven12<Inven1	-300.00		1940.00	5	Inven1	Inven12	Inven121	-375
9	9	Inven122<Inven12<Inven1	-170.00		1770.00	5	Inven1	Inven12	Inven122	-34
10	10	Inven221<Inven22<Inven2	3200.00		4970.00	10	Inven2	Inven22	Inven221	320
11	11	Inven222<Inven22<Inven2	5000.00		9970.00	10	Inven2	Inven22	Inven222	1000
12	12	PPUK parts<ASD parts<Inven2	4800.00		14770.00	10	Inven2	ASD parts	PPUK parts	1200
13	13	PPGH parts<ASD parts<Inven2	3800.00		18570.00	10	Inven2	ASD parts	PPGH parts	1900
14	14	Inven31<Inven3	5300.00		23870.00	10	Inven3	Inven31		530
15	15	Inven32<Inven3	2900.00		26770.00	10	Inven3	Inven32		580
16	16	Inven331<Inven33<Inven3	2700.00		29470.00	11	Inven3	Inven33	Inven331	1350
17	17	Inven332<Inven33<Inven3	3100.00		32570.00	11	Inven3	Inven33	Inven332	620

Query executed successfully. BENNY-PC\SQLEXPRESS (11.0 RTM) sa (53) jgp1 00:00:00 54 rows

Chapter 5

Accounting Future

Finally, I will introduce a concept of the great accounting, which is based on the MathAccounting software and the wealth conservation law, in detail. The great accounting means two aspects.

In the great data time, centered management of accounting is an inexorable trend. Every business company can login in a government's centered database by using of its business number. In addition, there is a famous law of the "Energy conservation law" in natural science. The every different exposition of this law has promoted science development. The most famous exposition of the law is atomic theory. Similarly, I think that there is a law of the "Wealth conservation law" in social science. All companies and organizations in the world will follow the law of the "Wealth conservation law". For a company or an organization, every department can do part work of the accounting about itself duty. All works of the company or the organization's departments will be made up of the financial statements. The great accounting has many advantages, such as being difficult to draw up false accounts and to evade a tax.

Now, the accounting department is too powerful. It not only manages cash, but also is responsible of being made up of the financial statements. However, many accounting data are second data which come from other departments. There may be some problems in the financial statements under the special circumstances. The accounting department's duty should be to manage the cash. Every department in a company or an organization can do part work of the accounting about itself duty. All works of the company or the organization's departments will be made up of the financial statements which are more reliable and correct.

5.1 Great accounting

The many expenses are related to every employee in a company or an organization, but the salary expenses is the most expense for every employee. Therefore, the form of the multi-subaccount name of the "Salary expenses" account should also be the same as the many expenses' accounts in the great accounting software.

If a company or an organization has 99 factories in the different places and the maximum number of every department's employees in a factory is 9999, then the three-level subaccount of the "Salary expenses" account is every employee ID which may be every employee's name, or phone number, or social insurance number. Its multi-subaccount's form is the "Employee ID<Different department <Different factory". If a company or an organization has only different departments, the multi-subaccount's form of the "Salary expenses" account is the "Employee ID<Different department".

The other many expenses can be distinguished from the salary expenses by adding a symbol of the "-xxxx". Its multi-subaccount's form is the "Employee ID-xxxx<Different department-xxxx<Different factory-xxxx". For example, the multi-subaccount's form of the "Other expenses" account is the "Employee name-other<Different department-other" in the Chapter 2.

The Figure 5-1 on the next page shows a typical company or organization structure which may have fifteen departments: accounting department, office department, human resource department, production department, equipment department, purchases department, sales department, inventory management department, research development department, and other departments. After clicking the fifteen boxes respectively, I get the same interface (seeing the Figure 5-2 on the next page). The accounting department can use four functions, seeing the first figure in the Figure 5-2. However, the other departments can only use transaction and report functions, seeing the second figure in the Figure 5-2. Then they can use the MathAccounting software to deal with themselves transactions.

The transaction function is same for every department. However, the report function has three situations: one for the accounting department, another one for the human resource department, and last one for other departments, seeing the Figure 5-3 which follows the

Figure 5-2. Every department can show all transactions in this paper. By adding a searching condition of the "Group by department", each department can only show itself transactions except for the accounting department.

The great accounting's data is the same as MathAccounting software in the following transactions. However, some expenses are distributed to every department, such as the "Supplies expenses" account. The "Supplies" account has two recording methods.

- The supplies are purchased by the purchases department and transferred into the inventory department. Then every department can pick up them and record its supplies expenses.

- Every department purchases its supplies and record its supplies expenses.

I use the second method for simplicity.

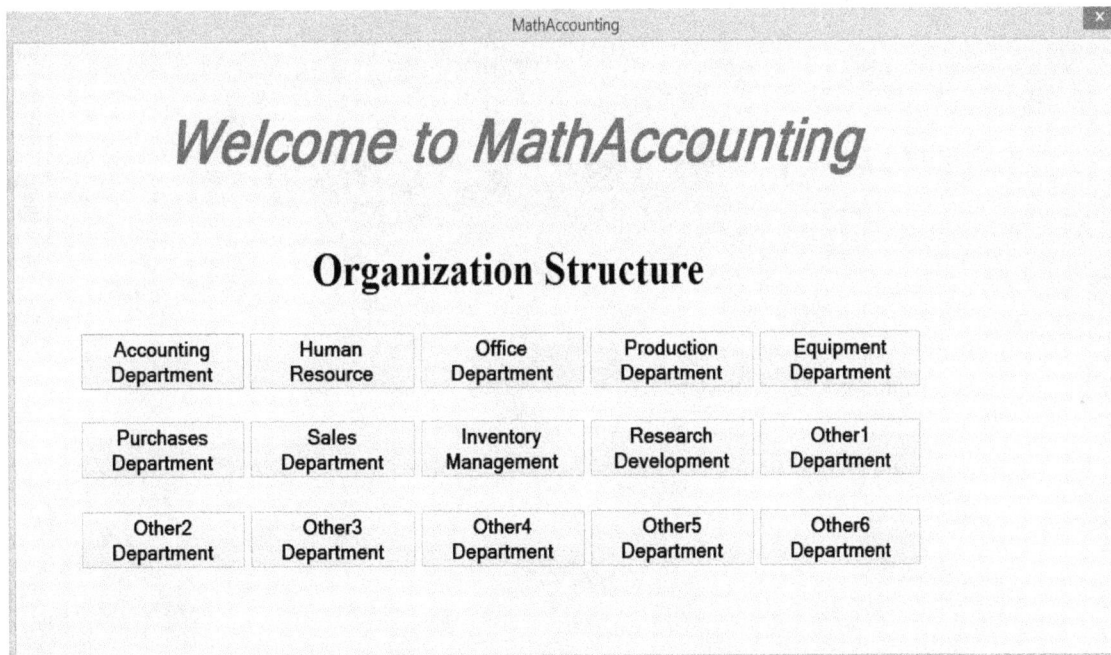

Figure 5-1   Organization Structure

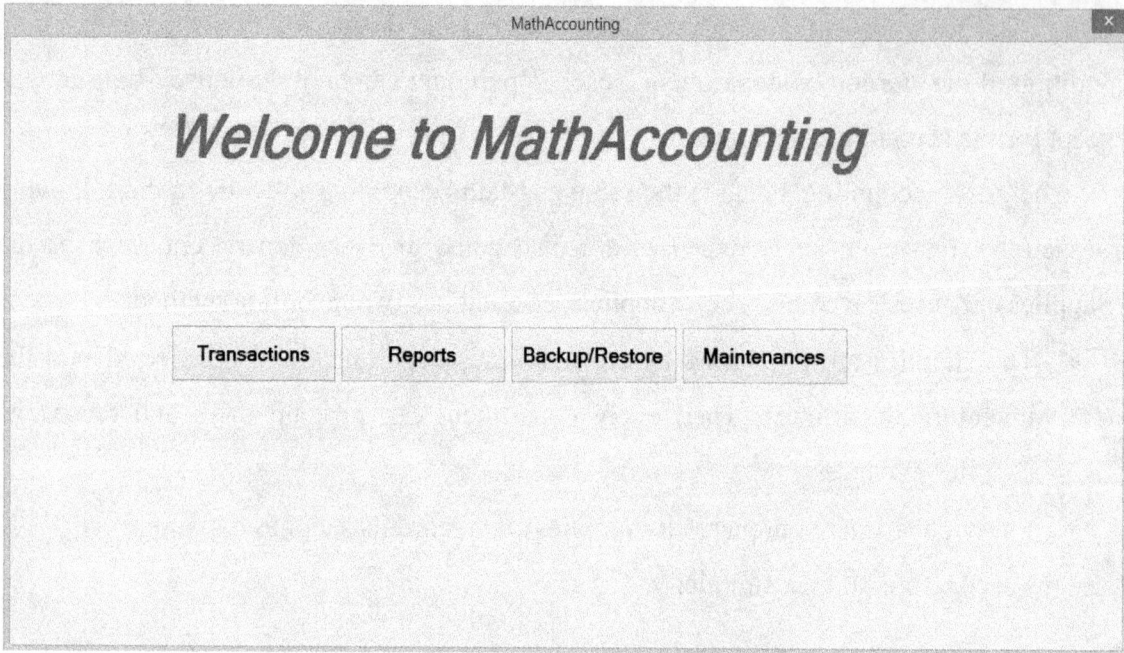

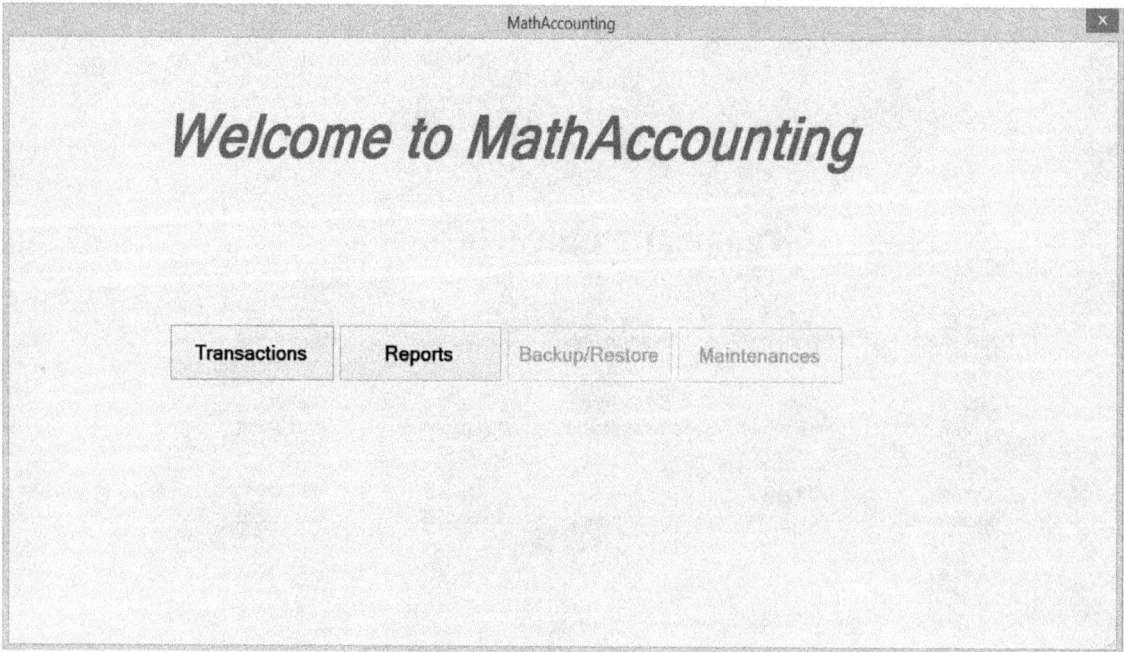

Figure 5-2   MathAccounting Interface

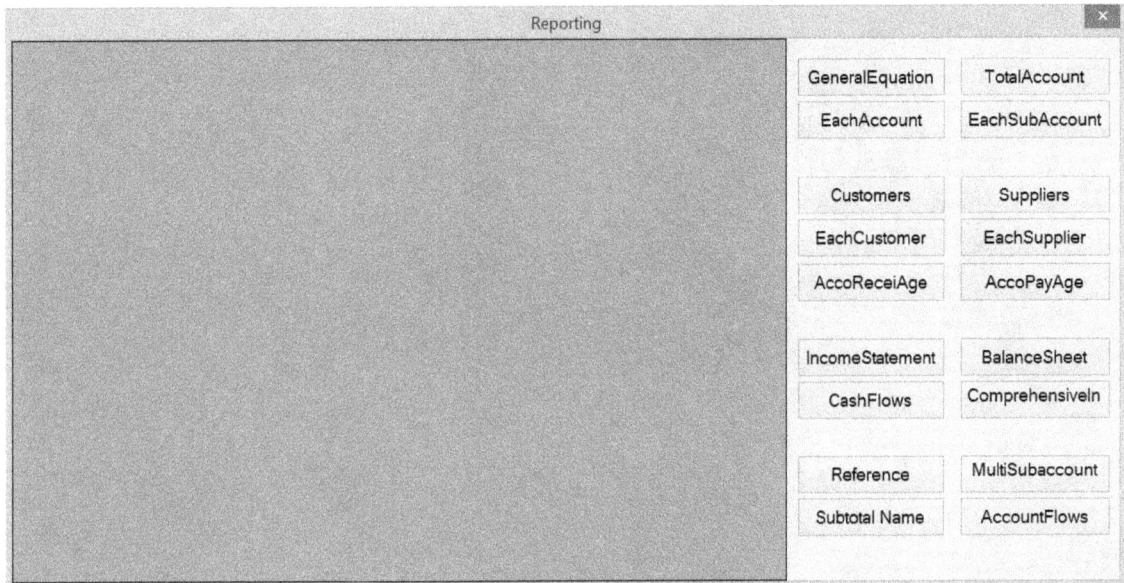

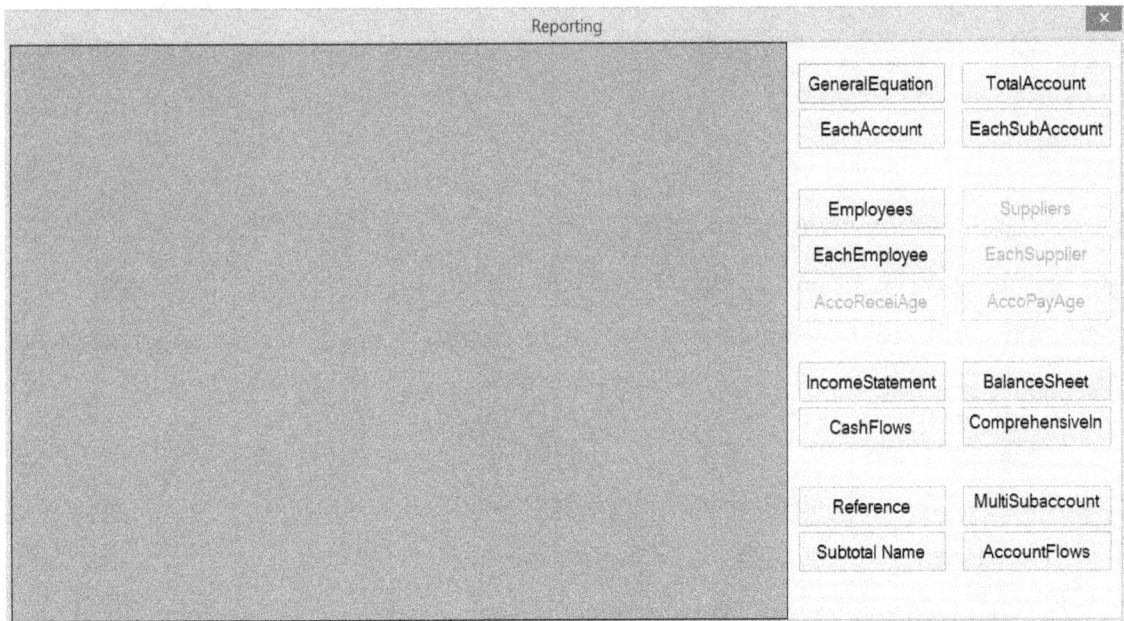

Figure 5-3   Report Interface (Continue)

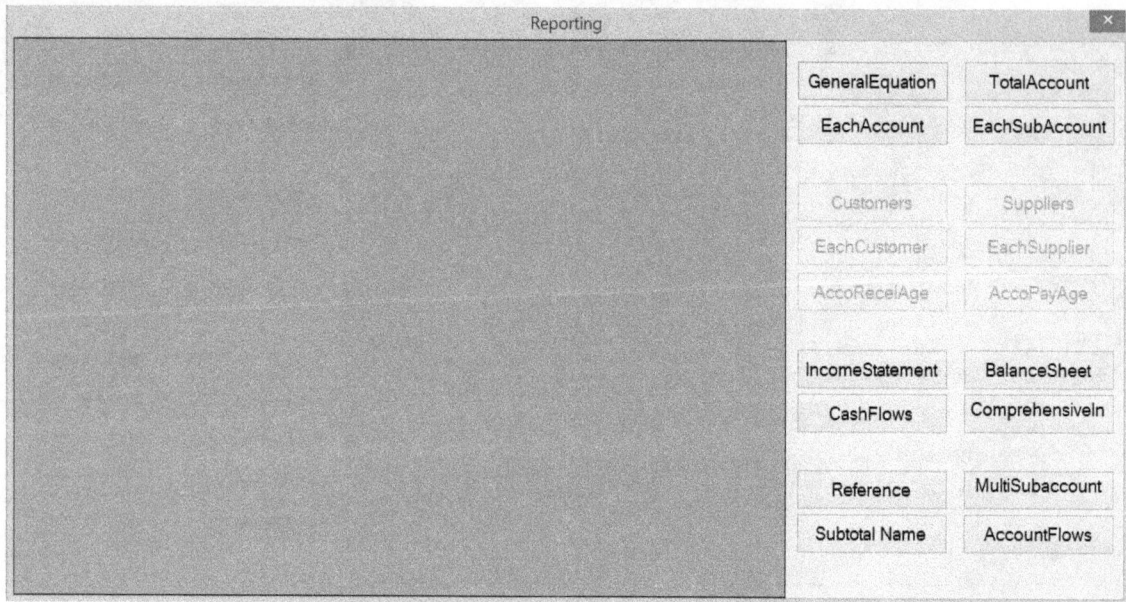

Figure 5-3   Report Interface

5.1.1 Accounting department

Accounting department duty is only to pay the cash according to the other departments' requirement except for recording itself salary expenses according to actual attendance and miscellaneous expenses.

Every employee's salary expenses is planned by the human resource department. According to actual attendance, some employees' actual salary expenses of the accounting department may be corrected by the accounting department.

If I do not wish too many expenses account appear in financial statements, I can use a parent account of the "Miscellaneous expenses" which may have the one-level subaccounts of the "Travelling expenses", the "Supplies expenses", and so on; the two-level subaccounts of the "Different department-travelling", the "Different department-supplies", and so on; the three-level subaccounts of the "Employee ID-travelling", the "Employee ID-supplies", and so on. The "Miscellaneous expenses payable" account has the one-level subaccounts of the "Employee ID-miscellaneous expenses payable".

5.1.2 Human resource department

The Human Resource department's main duty is to build every employee's profile including planned salary expenses and salary payable at beginning of every month. Of course, it also records itself salary expenses according to actual attendance and its miscellaneous expenses.

The "Salary expenses" account has the three-level subaccounts. Its multi-subaccount form should be the "Employee ID-salary<Different department-salary<Different factory-salary". However, the "Salary expenses" is the most expenses in all employee's expenses, so I define its multi-subaccount form as the "Employee ID<Different department<Different factory". The "Salary payable" account has the two-level subaccounts. Its multi-subaccount form is the "Employee ID-xxxx<XXXX payable". Here, I use the nature number as the employee ID. Of course, the employee's name or phone number or social insurance number is also used as the employee ID. In fact, the accounts of the "Travelling expenses" and the "Other expenses" accounts in the Chapter 2 and the Chapter 3 use the employee's name as the employee ID.

When entering a new employee ID which is a three-level subaccount of the parent account "Salary expenses" into the MultiSubaccount box, some boxes of employee's information are enabled. Then I can build this employee's profile, seeing the first figure in the Figure 5-4 which is on this page and the next page.

Transaction

Assets(1) = Liabilities(2) + Equity(3) + Incomes(4) - Expenses(5)

1/2/2014	Record an employee's profile	5	Salary expenses ⌄	-1250	1<Office department<First factory ⌄
Trans date	Explanation	Class	Account Name	Amount	MultiSubaccount Name

Operating and administrative e ⌄	454 ⌄	Ping Wang	Ping1	Ping2	Ping3	Ping4	3/1990	Ping5
Subtotal Name	Reference	Employee Name	Employee Address	E-mail	Phone	Gender	Birth Date	Bank Account

No.	TransDate	Class	Account Name	MultiSubaccount Name	Amouunt	
						Continue

Transaction

Assets(1) = Liabilities(2) + Equity(3) + Incomes(4) - Expenses(5)

1/2/2014	Record an employee's profile	2	Salary payable ⌄	1200	1-net payroll<Net payroll payable ⌄
Trans date	Explanation	Class	Account Name	Amount	MultiSubaccount Name

Current liability,203 ⌄	204 ⌄
Subtotal Name	Reference

No.	TransDate	Class	Account Name	MultiSubaccount Name	Amount	
1	1/2/2014	5	Salary expenses	1<Sales department<First factory	-1250	Continue

Figure 5-4   Record Employee Profile (Continue)

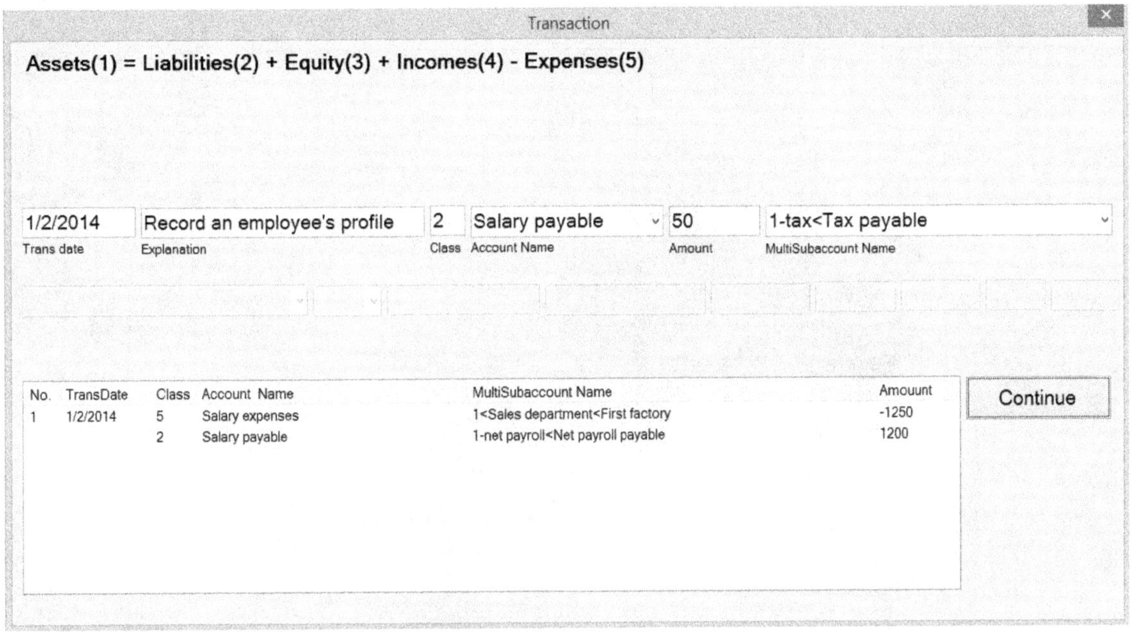

Figure 5-4 Record Employee Profile

The Figure 5-5 shows all employees' profile s (seeing the first figure) and one profile of the employee ID 3 (seeing the third figure).

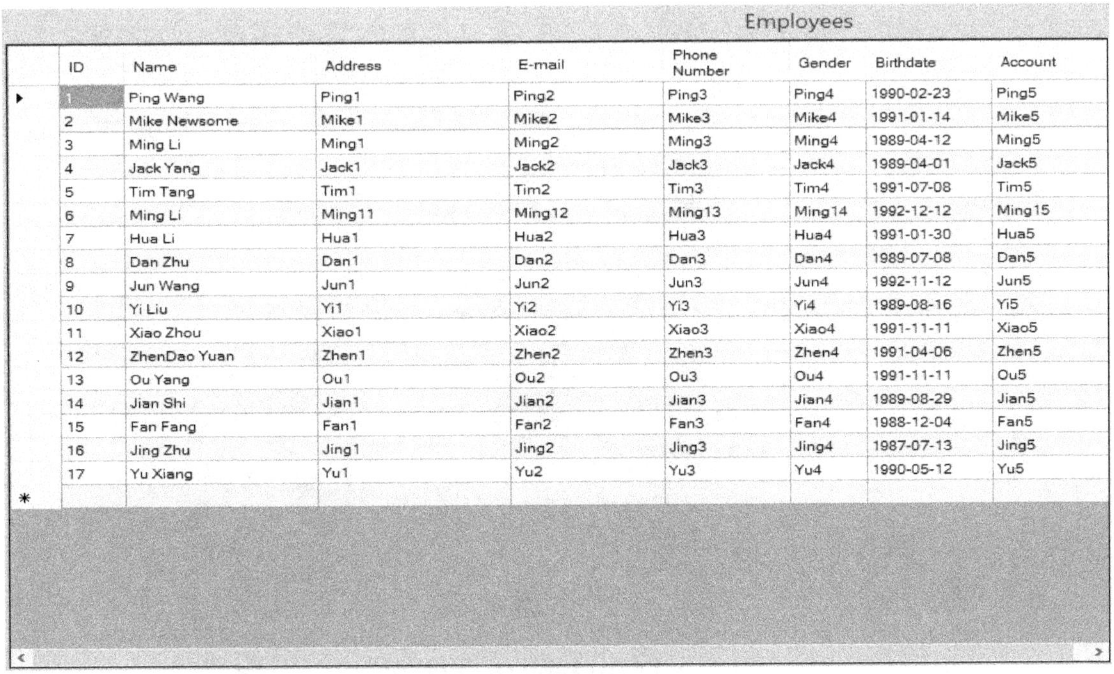

Employees

ID	Name	Address	E-mail	Phone Number	Gender	Birthdate	Account
1	Ping Wang	Ping1	Ping2	Ping3	Ping4	1990-02-23	Ping5
2	Mike Newsome	Mike1	Mike2	Mike3	Mike4	1991-01-14	Mike5
3	Ming Li	Ming1	Ming2	Ming3	Ming4	1989-04-12	Ming5
4	Jack Yang	Jack1	Jack2	Jack3	Jack4	1989-04-01	Jack5
5	Tim Tang	Tim1	Tim2	Tim3	Tim4	1991-07-08	Tim5
6	Ming Li	Ming11	Ming12	Ming13	Ming14	1992-12-12	Ming15
7	Hua Li	Hua1	Hua2	Hua3	Hua4	1991-01-30	Hua5
8	Dan Zhu	Dan1	Dan2	Dan3	Dan4	1989-07-08	Dan5
9	Jun Wang	Jun1	Jun2	Jun3	Jun4	1992-11-12	Jun5
10	Yi Liu	Yi1	Yi2	Yi3	Yi4	1989-08-16	Yi5
11	Xiao Zhou	Xiao1	Xiao2	Xiao3	Xiao4	1991-11-11	Xiao5
12	ZhenDao Yuan	Zhen1	Zhen2	Zhen3	Zhen4	1991-04-06	Zhen5
13	Ou Yang	Ou1	Ou2	Ou3	Ou4	1991-11-11	Ou5
14	Jian Shi	Jian1	Jian2	Jian3	Jian4	1989-08-29	Jian5
15	Fan Fang	Fan1	Fan2	Fan3	Fan4	1988-12-04	Fan5
16	Jing Zhu	Jing1	Jing2	Jing3	Jing4	1987-07-13	Jing5
17	Yu Xiang	Yu1	Yu2	Yu3	Yu4	1990-05-12	Yu5

Figure 5-5 All Employees Profiles (Continue)

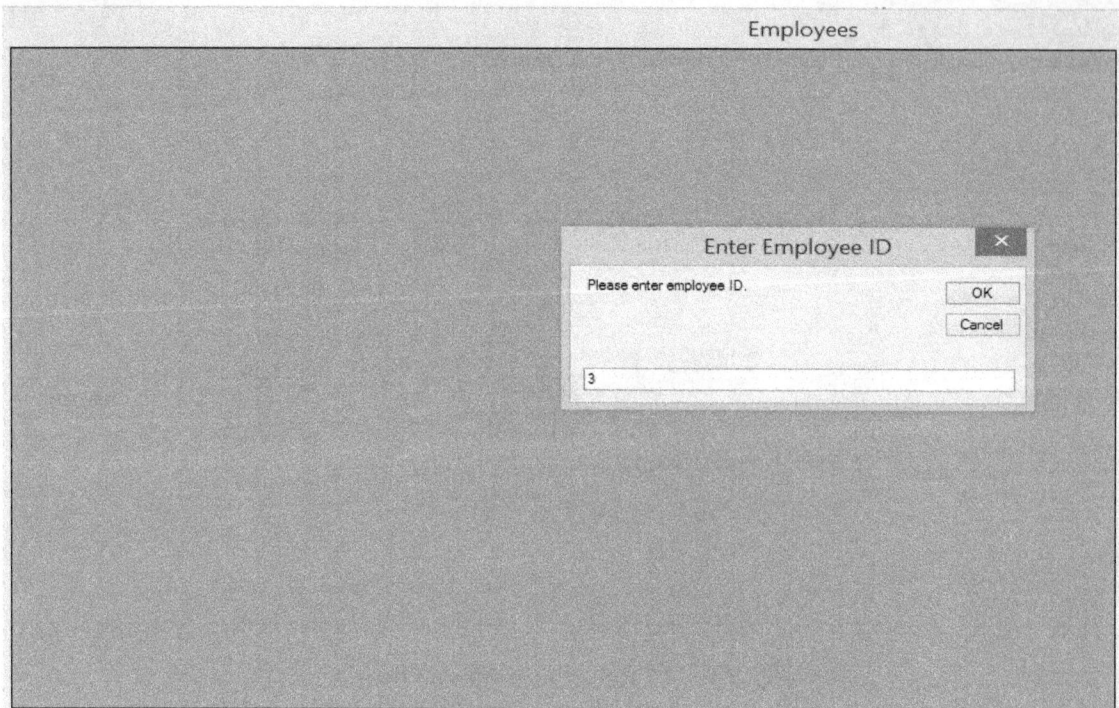

Figure 5-5   All Employees Profiles

5.1.3 Office department

Office department duty is to record itself salary expenses according to actual attendance and its miscellaneous expenses.

5.1.4 Production department

Production department duty is to record the inventory in production process except for recording itself salary expenses according to actual attendance and its miscellaneous expenses.

5.1.5 Equipment department

Equipment department duty is to record the amortization expenses and accumulated amortization except for recording itself salary expenses according to actual attendance and its miscellaneous expenses.

5.1.6 Purchases department

Purchase department duty is to record and manage the account payable and the suppliers' information except for recording itself salary expenses according to actual attendance and its miscellaneous expenses.

5.1.7 Sales department

Sales department duty is to record and manage the account receivable and the customers' information except for recording itself salary expenses according to actual attendance and its miscellaneous expenses.

5.1.8 Inventory department

Inventory department duty is to record and manage the inventory according to other departments' needs except for recording itself salary expenses according to actual attendance and its miscellaneous expenses.

5.1.9 Research development department

Research development department duty is to record the research development expenses except for recording itself salary expenses according to actual attendance and its miscellaneous expenses.

5.2 Sample of an accounting fiscal year

Last thing is to enter more transactions to complete an accounting fiscal year. During entering these transactions in the Chapter 2 and Chapter 3, I use the different department's model to deal with itself related transactions. Finally, I get the five tables: Income Statement, Balance Sheet, Cash Flows Statement, Comprehensive Income Statement, and Account Flows Statement which are the same as the chapter 3.

REFERENCES

[WK] Jerry J. Weygandt, Donald E.Kieso, Pau D.Kimmel, Barbara Trenholm, and Valerie A. Kinnear, *Accounting Principles Part 1* 4th Canadian ed. John Wiley & Sons Canada, Ltd. Ontario, 2007.

[WK] Jerry J. Weygandt, Donald E.Kieso, Pau D.Kimmel, Barbara Trenholm, and Valerie A. Kinnear, *Accounting Principle Part 2s* 4th Canadian ed. John Wiley & Sons Canada, Ltd. Ontario, 2007.

[WK] Jerry J. Weygandt, Donald E.Kieso, Pau D.Kimmel, Barbara Trenholm, and Valerie A. Kinnear, *Accounting Principles Part 3* 4th Canadian ed. John Wiley & Sons Canada, Ltd. Ontario, 2007.

[KW] Donald E. Kieso, Jerry J. Weygandt, Terry D. Warfield, Nicola M. Young, and Irene M. Wiecek, *Intermediate Accounting Volume 1* 8th Canadian ed. John Wiley & Sons Canada, Ltd. Ontario, 2007.

[KW] Donald E. Kieso, Jerry J. Weygandt, Terry D. Warfield, Nicola M. Young, and Irene M. Wiecek, *Intermediate Accounting Volume 2* 8th Canadian ed. John Wiley & Sons Canada, Ltd. Ontario, 2007.